THE GLORY
OF THE
HOLY TRINITY

is ours if only we'll believe in Christ and put our trust in Him, and receive His Spirit. God the Holy Spirit has come to us from Heaven, at Christ's bidding, sent by the Father to make us His adopted sons and daughters; and whoever believes this can see that God in Three Persons has a marvellous plan, which is to gather us together and to make us one family - one 'Body' - in Christ.

A PERSONAL CHOICE.

The whole Trinity, one God, is at work to give us joy, if only we'll trust in God, and try to do His Will, not our own; and those of us who have 'met' God have sometimes wept for grief that we have ever tried to live without Him, or have ever failed to trust in His goodness; and this is because we've learned that we frail creatures are loved by God with a fervour and intensity which cannot be equalled elsewhere. He longs to bring each one of us into an intimate friendship with Himself, and at the same time to gather us together and to heal the divisions caused by our sinfulness; and that's why Christ is still at work today, in His Church, through the Spirit's power and guidance, reaching out again and again, calling men and women, and children too, to be reconciled with their Heavenly Father.

Through the Sacraments of Baptism, Confirmation and Holy Eucharist we can be freed from sin and made full members of the Catholic Church.

SHARING THE GOOD NEWS.

What the Church has taught me, and I have believed, I now know from experience: that, through Christ, we can have a share in the life of the Holy Trinity; and we are given the sure hope of being able to enjoy that life of perfect peace and joy in Eternity, if we remain faithful; and so I'm glad to be able to say, in words and pictures, in this book and in several others: "God is Good! God is gloriously alive and loving and beautiful. Never doubt this, but believe in Him, and accept His invitation. Go to meet Him in prayer, and in the sacraments of His Church, and in the lives of your brothers and sisters. Give up sin, by His grace, and try to do good; and if you fail, go and be reconciled, and trust in God's love, and begin again, in simplicity and humility".

"IN THEIR OWN LANGUAGE".

I've known, for a long time, that Christ wants me to give a little 'glimpse' of His Divine life and work and glory, using images as well as words; but it was only today that He showed me clearly the significance of the paintings I've produced at His request - based on the images which He has given to me in prayer. He reminded me about the missionary work of certain persons who approached a new community, to speak of Divine love, and whose preaching of the Gospel was effective because "they preached to them in their own language." Christ has told me that, for many people, images are the 'language' of our age.

A WORLD OF IMAGERY.

Millions of people take in information from day to day and year to year not by reading but by absorbing what they find in images: through adverts, through non-stop TV programmes, through DVD players, picture-magazines, pop-videos and photo-journalism; and so Christ wants to present even a subject like this - the life and work of the Holy Trinity - in a picture language which can be easily digested: though there's a text as well, for people who also like to read.

GOD: TRANSCENDENT AND INVISIBLE.

Having just written about producing 'pictures' of the Holy Trinity, I must appear to contradict myself by agreeing with people who assert that none of us can know what God in Three Persons looks like.

We cannot see God, in this life, as one sees an object; and even in eternal life, we can suppose, our spiritual 'sight' cannot encompass, all-at-once, the infinite beauty and majesty of our Creator: of the Three-in-One Who has made us and Who is willing to transform us.

It's true, however, that Christ became Incarnate; and He has revealed Himself to the eyes of my soul in prayer, on many occasions. He has shown me His glory, and has led me to see the glory, also, of the Father and of the Holy Spirit; and if I refuse to acknowledge this privilege I shall fail to praise God's generosity and goodness; and so I'm pleased to have a new opportunity of writing about Him and of sharing some of the images which He has given me in prayer, and which I've placed within this book in chronological order.

A WISE TEACHER.

Every illustration within this book has been taken from a lengthy series of teachings which I've received from Christ about the human soul, and about the spiritual journey which we are invited to make 'in Christ' through purification to union.

Christ has helped me in my own journey in a hundred thousand ways; and now I know that just as a teacher holds up before his pupil an image of a far-off country, or a diagram of a nearby work-place, in order to stimulate greater interest and to provide further details about a topic or project, so Christ has 'held up' to me glimpses and images of His work and of His glory; and now He holds up those images through me, for other people, to stimulate greater interest in the life and work of the Godhead which is our Origin, our Source of love and hope and power, and our eternal home.

THE GREAT JUBILEE.

Christ has also shown me that this book will serve as a memento of our recent Holy Year: our year of Jubilee.

Christ has looked on with delight, as we have celebrated approximately the two thousandth anniversary of His Incarnation; and because the Jubilee Year was dedicated to the Most Holy Trinity, Christ has asked me to publish this book of paintings in His honour, and to honour the Father and the Holy Spirit - and to bring encouragement to all who are glad to call themselves His brothers and sisters: members of His Church on earth, and heirs to the Kingdom.

15 February 2001
Saints Cyril and Methodius.

THE GLORY
OF THE
HOLY TRINITY

A GLIMPSE OF HIS GLORY.

If we are new to the Christian life, we sometimes come before God in prayer, through Christ, with a daunting awareness of our sinfulness; and we are amazed that we have found the courage to approach the All-Holy. Yet we are right to believe in God's love. All who approach God in trust and reverent worship can hope to be led further 'towards' Him, through His Providential care. For our happiness, God longs to transform us in the pure fire of His holiness; yet He is patient and gentle; and as we grow in faith and hope and love we will grow in the conviction that we really belong to Him, and that, through our Baptism, the Holy Trinity dwells within our souls - whether we now experience that presence or still wait and trust in darkness of soul.

The figure in the picture opposite represents not a newcomer to the spiritual life, but someone who has been making her way steadily up the 'holy mountain' (Ps 48:1): someone who has persevered through the dark times: someone who has tried to endure with love not only the miseries and torments which we meet in earthly life, amidst sweet surprises and piercing joys, but also the 'nights' of the soul.

To emerge from those 'nights' after a brief stripping-of-the-soul of all illusions and selfish attachments, or after a long and penitential cleansing in the burning fire of 'naked' exposure of self to God, in prayer, is to be dazzled by beauty and light. The soul meets the Divine light. She 'enters' it in prayer, free at last from perpetual remorse, yet awe-struck at her first glimpse of the glory of the Holy Trinity. Now she can say, from experience, that she is held and embraced by the Holy Trinity, in her everyday life, amidst her many weaknesses. She trusts in God's compassionate love; and so she longs to grow stronger in faith and hope and love, until the day when she enters Heaven. She longs to live within the Holy and glorious Trinity forever, as if within the triple flame which burns in glory with one, holy light.

(Text adapted from *Teachings in Prayer Volume One*, T:50 of 1986)

The soul is awe-struck, on seeing something of the Triune Glory.
(OIL-S:50)

3

THE OCEAN OF DIVINE LOVE.

Someone who is fascinated by God, and who longs to know Him, will realise before long that friendship can grow only through regular meetings and conversations; and because God is pure and all-holy whereas we are weak and sinful, those conversations should include expressions of sorrow for sin, as well as thanks for all the gifts we take for granted, with words of homage and adoration, of the sort which are due from a creature to his Creator.

Such reverent and loving expressions are the 'debt' which we all owe to God, so to speak, whether our souls are on fire with love, or grey with grief - or overburdened with doubts or earthly sadnesses.

Truly, God exists, still. He loves us, always; and if we have 'a mustard-seed' of true faith (Mt 17:20) we'll know that every prayer is worthwhile. Every prayer is precious, and is welcomed by God. By every word of sincere prayer, whether in darkness or light, we bind ourselves closer to God, or, rather, we allow Him to draw us closer to Himself; and we grow in virtue. We can't fail to benefit, each time we turn to God our Father in prayer, in Christ's name and by His Spirit, and abandon ourselves to His Will.

The picture illustrates the fact that it's as if we 'fall' into the embrace of the Holy Trinity with every movement of our hearts in prayer. Though we might meet no sight, sound or touch, and are genuinely content to live by faith, we are sometimes aware of God's presence, or of the power by which He upholds us.

(Text adapted from *Teachings in Prayer Volume One*, T:65 of Summer 1986)

By surrender to God in prayer, the soul
enters the embrace of the Holy Trinity.
(OIL-S:65)

5

A VAST HALL OF LIGHT.

We live by faith. We cannot yet see God, nor is it usual for us to see the Saints who live 'in' God, in glory. As members of the Church, however, we are in communion with everyone in the Church, which consists of our brothers and sisters in the Church on earth, and the Holy Souls who are being purified after death, and also the Saints in Heaven; so we can be sure that whenever we turn to God in prayer, we are turning to the Saints at the same time; and whenever we address one of our Saintly friends in Heaven to ask for prayers, we are turning to God at the same time, since each Saint lives 'in' Him.

The illustration shows what we can imagine is happening when we turn to God in sincere prayer, perhaps to intercede for a sick friend - or perhaps simply to thank Him for the gifts we take for granted.

It's as though, by looking within ourselves in prayer, and by speaking to God the Father in the name of Christ, we have allowed the Holy Spirit to draw us into a vast 'Hall of light'. There, in the presence of the Holy Trinity, and in the company of the Saints, we can speak like children about our gratitude - or our sorrows or sins; or we can pray for other people by lifting them into God's light, so to speak, by a word, a thought or a pang. They are 'bathed' in God's graces, and renewed in mysterious ways, through our intercession - if they don't deliberately shut the door to His gifts.

(Text adapted from *Teachings in Prayer Volume One*, T:67 of 24.8.86)

By looking within our own souls, in prayer,
we can encounter God, and the Saints.
(OIL-S:67)

INTO THE THREE-FOLD LOVE.

We need not talk to God unceasingly when we turn to Him in prayer. By our response to the prompting of the Holy Spirit, we have entered the Divine embrace as we pray in the name of Jesus to our Father in Heaven. We are loved not by an impersonal Force, but by Three Persons - One God - Whose very nature is love and mercy and compassion. They long to enfold us forever in the depths of Their embrace, when we have given up our sinful ways, and have lived entirely for Their glory and have finished our work on earth.

Whether we are contented or ill-at-ease in everyday life, we have only to step 'into the depths' of God, through prayer, in order to receive God's help; and there's no need for us to worry about our distractions. We can lessen these, to some extent, if we lead calmer lives or if we can make time to 'settle down' before we begin our prayer; but meanwhile, we know, by faith, that we are held in the life and love of the Most Holy Trinity - even when all seems to be silence and darkness.

If we remain patient and faithful - whether for many months or many years - we might be drawn, at a time of God's choosing, into the true prayer of 'unknowing': drawn by God's invitation and by Divine power into the very life of God. It's as if we are entwined within the love of the Three Divine Persons, the Holy Trinity: as if far above earth's limitations.

(Text adapted from *Teachings in Prayer Volume One,* T:68 of August 1986)

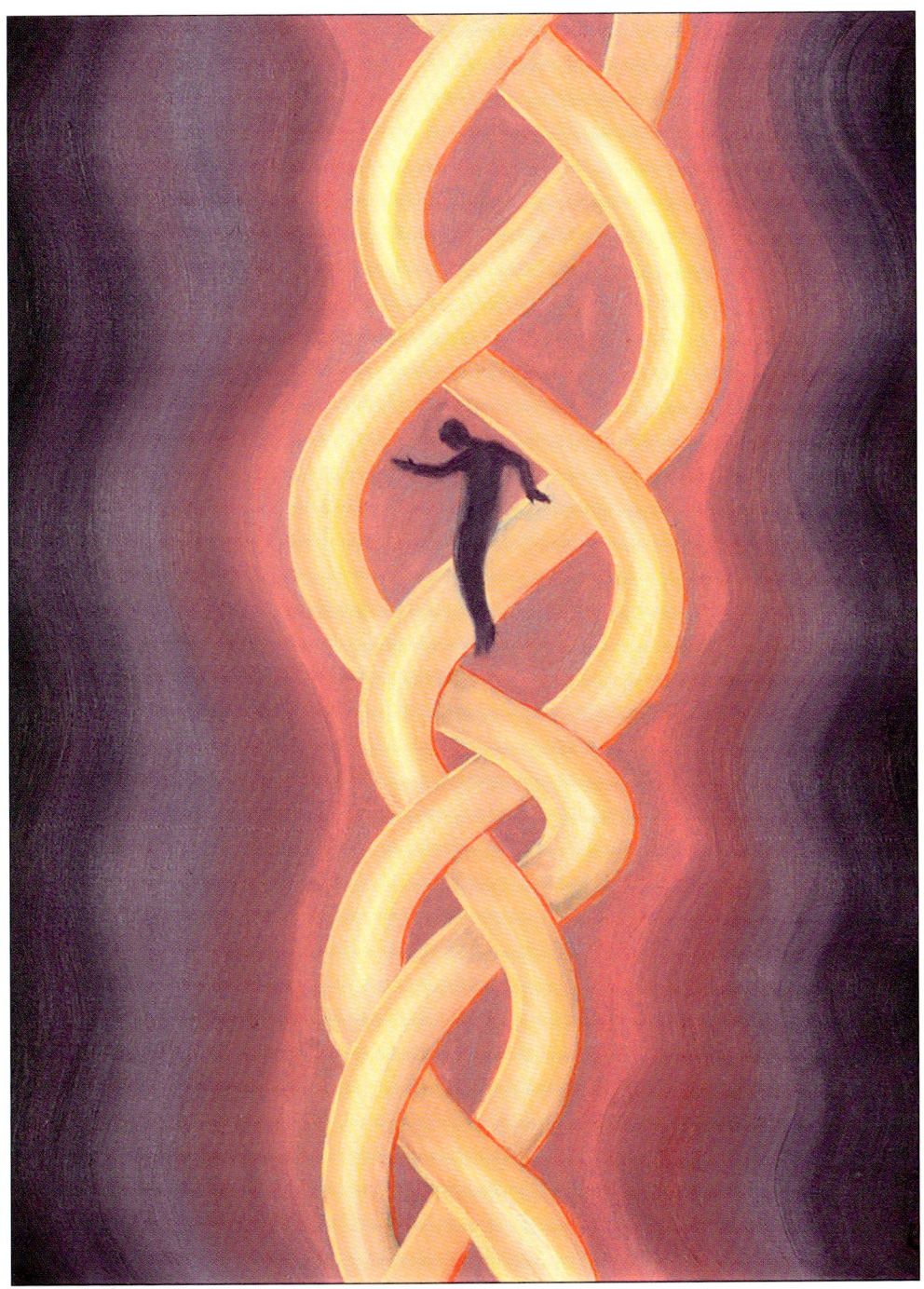

The soul who is drawn into 'Unknowing'
prayer is held within the Triune love.
(OIL-S:68B)

HELD IN GOD'S LOVE.

How amazing it is, that God is love, and that He invites us to live within His life of unceasing love, first through our faith and Baptism and in the union of Holy Communion, and then - as He draws the soul towards Himself in contemplative union - in prayer, and at the end of our lives in Heaven. What more could He do for us? How astonishing it is that we have ever complained about His requests, or about His care for us.

At every moment of our lives - if we have been reconciled to God - we are guided by the Holy Spirit, though remaining free to ignore His promptings; and we're also nourished by Christ in His sacraments, so living and maturing as true children of the Father; and in this enviable state we need never give into despondency or doubt.

If we cling, through faith, to the knowledge that God's love for us is constant and powerful, whether we experience dryness in prayer or fleeting moments of glory or sweetness, we can develop a deep interior peace.

If we entrust ourselves to God, we can be confident that we live 'in' God at all times and in all places, whether we are busy at work or occupied with prayer, at home or abroad. We can be sure that wherever we go, our Heavenly Father always 'surrounds' us, Jesus is our constant companion, and the Holy Spirit Who inspires every good thought we have can uphold us and keep us faithful to the end.

(Text adapted from *Teachings in Prayer Volume One*, T:110 of 24.3.87)

At home, or away, we are always held,
accompanied and inspired by the Holy Trinity.
(OIL-S:110)

INTO THE DANCE OF ETERNITY.

From the lives and words of our spiritual ancestors we have learned that the joys and rewards of the spiritual life are so great that those who discover them are perpetually on fire with gratitude and joy.

Such gifts are scarcely believed in, however, by people whose souls are still veiled in darkness, and who cry out for consolation yet who seem to receive no answers to their prayers.

Many of those who climb valiantly towards Heaven through their devotion to God and their selfless love for their neighbours have not yet proved that they love God more than they love His gifts; and only when they have persevered in prayer through the months or years of necessary testing do they receive from God - those few who haven't abandoned the path - proofs of intimate friendship. Then they receive astonishing rewards for their love and for their labours.

At times of God's choosing, the willing soul can be lifted towards Heaven, in prayer, by God's power. It's as if that soul is 'spiralling' into Eternity, in the 'embrace' of the Holy Trinity, and is led into the 'dance' of all who live in love forever: into the dance of God's friends, the Saints and the Holy Angels.

(Text adapted from *Teachings in Prayer Volume One*, T:259 of 11.6.88)

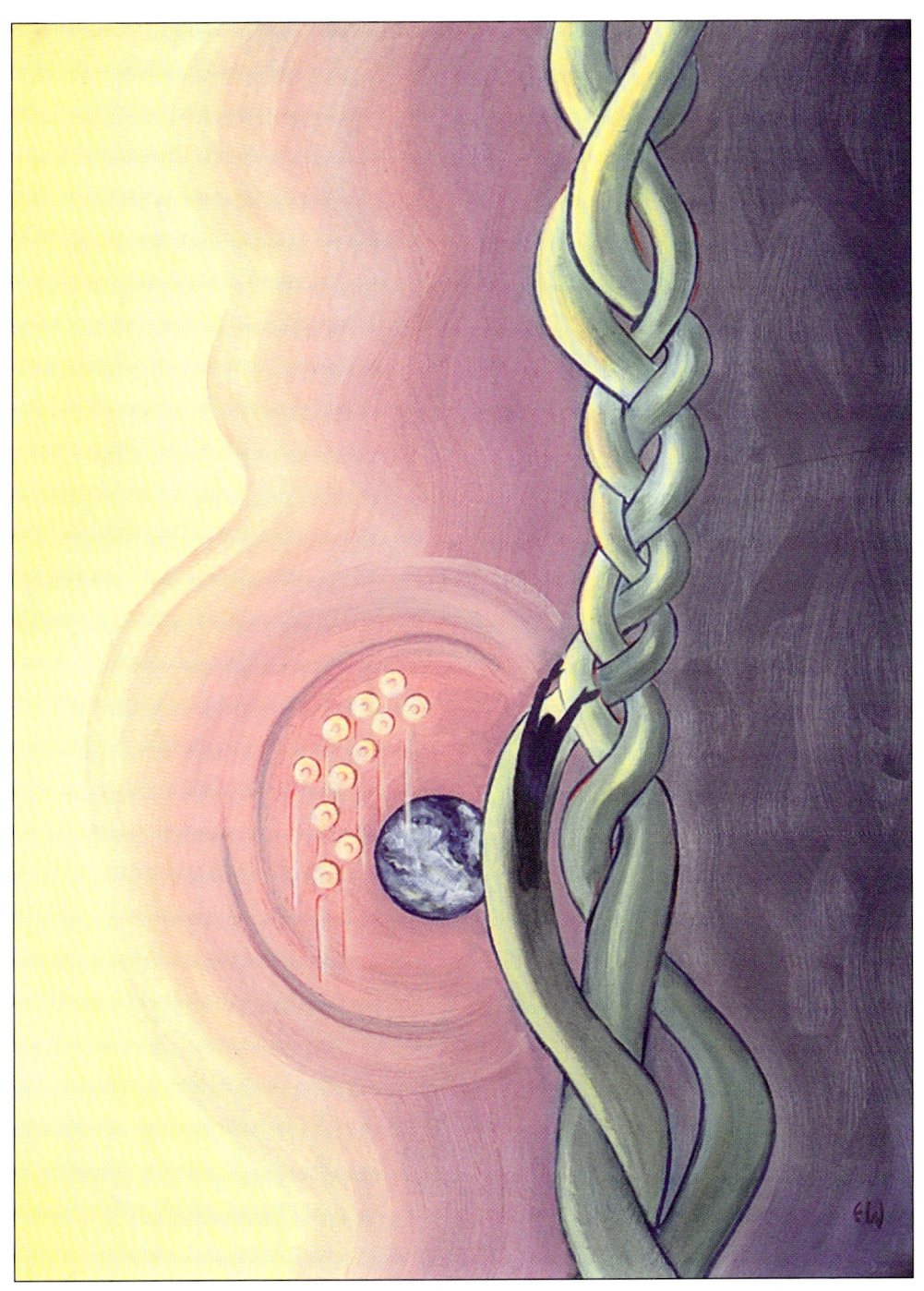

*At times of God's choosing, the soul is led
'spiralling' in prayer, into the dance of Eternity.
(OIL-S:259)*

BY HIS SPIRIT'S POWER.

Christ's frequent message to us all, through the Gospels, is: 'There is no need to be afraid' (Mt 10:31). His love cannot harm us; yet we shall meet opposition, if we are determined to follow His Way; and we shall be tempted to become disheartened by the knowledge of His purity and our sinfulness. He can bring us through all dangers, however, to the point where our will is the same as His Will.

When our whole desire is for the good of our neighbour, and the glory of the Father, our prayer will be very simple. We shall make one prayer with Christ, offering ourselves with and through Him to the Father, both in private prayer and in the Sacred Liturgy of the Church; and one day we shall find that we rise up in spirit, in prayer: as if drawn by a mighty power.

More and more frequently we find that if we approach Christ in trust and confidence, He lifts us - after our purifications and by His Spirit's power - into His own Heavenly prayer, which is welcomed by the Father.

Freed from sin and anxiety, we are one with Christ in praise and thanksgiving, amongst the Saints and Holy Angels; and we find that whenever we pray, in joyful surrender, we can follow Christ to the heart of the Holy Trinity.

(Text adapted from *Teachings in Prayer Volume One,* T:290 of 15.11.80)

*After various purifications, the soul is lifted
by Christ into His own prayer to the Father.
(OIL-S:290)*

15

THE INTERIOR UNIVERSE.

God the Father holds everything in existence. Everything that exists lies within His love. Jesus is the sweetest and kindest friend and lover; and the Holy Spirit continually holds and soothes and strengthens all who have allowed Him to draw near and to enter their hearts.

The closer is our friendship with God, the surer becomes our trust in His loving presence near us. It gives us joy to visit shrines and holy places, and to enter our church which has been consecrated for the celebration of the Sacred Mysteries, yet we know that God is everywhere. We are never abandoned, however great our faults or deep our weariness; and we can look within ourselves, in order to find God. We can enter our 'secret place' (Mt 6:6) in order to pray, as if entering a sanctuary.

Like the person in the picture, we can look upon our soul's 'centre' as being a 'place' which is vaster than any place we might see with our bodily eyes. Within this interior universe, we can meet the Holy Trinity in prayer. We know that the Father's concern for us is the unending, the Spirit's perpetual task is to draw us up to the Father, as Christ reaches out to us in many ways, to feed us and to reassure us of His love; and so we can worship in peace and gratitude. The soul which is full of Divine life is a 'place' on earth where God is First and Last - 'the Alpha and the Omega' (Rv 22:13). It is a place where God has been enthroned and adored by someone who consents to do His Will and permits Him to reign in every detail of life. If we live 'in' God, wholly united to Him in heart, mind and intentions, at the heart of the Holy Trinity, we are assured of love, grace, and safety; and to 'live 'in' God is to be saturated not just with love but also with knowledge from God: knowledge given within the light in which the Three Divine Persons live: the light in which They contemplate Their own being.

(Text adapted from *Teachings in Prayer Volume One*, T:461 of 7.8.90)

A soul which is full of love for God is a
'place' which is flooded with Divine light.
(OIL-S:461)

PRAYER RISING LIKE INCENSE.

Someone who loves God and trusts in Him thanks and praises Him, and peacefully repents of sins - and also asks with confidence for good things, both material and spiritual.

We've learned to pray, in the 'Our Father': 'Give us this day our daily bread;' and Christ our God tells us, in Holy Scripture, that it is important to persevere in prayer - and that God our Father Who is good will give us greater gifts that we'd receive from a sinful man. Christ rewarded with healing many people who asked for help; and St. James tells us: 'If any one of you is in trouble, he should pray' (Jm 5:13); and he also says: 'When you do pray and don't get it, it is because you have not prayed properly' (Jm 4:3). So we can picture our petitions for ourselves, and our intercessions for other people, as being pleasing to God, Who delights in our trust and loves to shower His gifts upon us.

Sad to say, there are innumerable and comforting gifts and graces we cannot receive if we never pray to God, or don't trust Him. This is not to say that He chooses to ignore us; rather, by our pride or lack of belief or trust we can shut Him out of our lives, thereby closing the door to many blessings, the greatest of which is eternal life.

When we pray to the Father in Christ's name, in the Holy Spirit, we can be confident that our prayers are heard.

The picture reminds us that when we love God, and have a living faith in His love, we know that every prayer we pray for our friends and relations - living or departed - surges upwards, as if on a cloud of incense, to the height of Heaven, to where Christ reigns as true King, with the Father and the Holy Spirit.

(Text adapted from *Teachings in Prayer Volume One*, T:481 of 9.9.89)

Our sincere petitions and intercessions rise
up to God, Who welcomes and hears them.
(OIL-S:481A)

19

GATHERED TOGETHER.

A well-known phrase used by Christians is that "there's no such thing as private prayer." This is true, in the sense that every prayer we pray to the Father is offered in the name of Christ, in the Holy Spirit, whilst we pray, speak, and love as living members of Christ's Body, the Church.

We are 'in communion' with every other member of the Church who is in a state of grace: both with the living and the Faithful Departed; and if our desire is to love God and our neighbour, and if our prayer is to be able to do good and to avoid evil, and to have what we need to achieve those aims, then the prayers we pray 'in private' are, in essence, the same as the perpetual prayer of Christ and the prayers of all other true children of God.

It's through the sacraments - through Baptism, Confirmation and the Holy Eucharist - that we have been freed from sin and fully initiated into the 'People of God': into Christ's one, holy, Catholic Church; and because we are in Communion with Christ and in full Communion with one another we are bound together as one offering with Christ to the Father, at the Holy Sacrifice of the Mass, which is the greatest act of worship of God that can be found on earth.

As we meet to take part in the Sacred Mysteries, we offer ourselves with Christ, in prayer. The Holy Spirit 'girdles' us by His power - or binds us together as a sheaf of corn is bound at the harvest; and so He increases our bond of unity as the one Body of Christ; indeed, He is that bond. He is the love which unites us; and through our union with Christ Who is Really Present amongst us after the Consecration we make one sacrifice of praise to the Father of glory: a prayer so glorious, obedient and powerful that it 'pierces' Heaven.

(Text adapted from *Teachings in Prayer Volume One,* T:493 of 17.10.89)

*The Holy Spirit binds together Christ's
friends, uniting them to Him, in the Mass.
(OIL-S:493A)*

21

JEWELS ON HIS ROBE.

Every Mass is a marvel of Divine love; and we who take part are privileged beyond our greatest imaginings. Only God Who is all-loving and all-holy could have devised a memorial celebration which is all-at-once a reminder of His gradual Revelation of Himself to the Chosen People, a re-enactment of what Christ did for us before He was betrayed and sent to His death, a living memorial of Christ's death and Resurrection and Ascension, a foretaste of the feasting which Christ's friends share in Heaven, a spiritual communion with those dear friends of Christ's who have already left earthly life to enter the safety of Purgatory or the glory of Heaven - and a real Communion with the living Lord Himself: with Jesus.

All of this is achieved through the power of the Holy Spirit, as He works through the words of Christ which are spoken by our priest - our 'alter Christus' amongst us - over a little piece of unleavened bread and a cup of wine. Bread and wine are changed to become Christ's own Sacred Body and Blood - with His soul and Divinity. Christ our Lord is present 'whole and entire', in a sacramental manner (CCC:1377); and through our regular participation in the Holy Sacrifice of the Mass, we allow Christ to draw us steadily towards Heaven: towards the heart of the Holy Trinity.

In the painting, Christ wears a chasuble which is adorned with a cross. He looks upwards, in love. It's as though He holds out His arms in utter surrender to the Father and offers the Holy Sacrifice on our behalf; and we who love Christ and who cling to Him, not just in everyday life but also in the Sacred Liturgy, as we make the offering with Christ, are like jewels on Christ's robe. By our loving union of ourselves with Christ, as He prays in our presence, we give honour to Christ, and make a unique adornment of His praise of the Father's glory.

(Text adapted from *Teachings in Prayer Volume One*, T:535 of 14.1.90)

Those who praise the Father with and through Christ are like jewels on Christ's priestly robe.
(OIL-S:535)

23

A DOOR-WAY TO GLORY.

Even when we are living 'in Christ,' trying to love Him and our neighbour, few of us are entirely without fear when we think about death and bereavement; yet if we believe in God, and have tried to come out 'into the light' (Jn 3:21) rather than to hide from God in sin and darkness, we can hope to be made happy in the eternal light, when we die.

There, we can meet the Father Who has created us, the Son Who has died for our sake, and the Holy Spirit Who has guided us safely to our true 'homeland' (Ph 3:20).

The sick person in the painting is huddled on a bed, not knowing what lies behind the 'wall' which represents the last day of an earthly life-time - or the 'edge' of Eternity.

Whatever sort of life this person has led, she will go through a 'door', so to speak, by passing from this life to the next. In the 'light' or wisdom of God, she will see her own life and actions and intentions laid bare with perfect clarity.

If she has shunned God's light and love, in earthly life, she will not be forced into glory, but will choose to turn away from light, and from joy; but if she is already one of God's 'children of light' she will praise and adore God for having forgiven her sins, and for having brought her to know His love, and His beauty, and for allowing her to live with Him forever, in joy and glory.

(Text adapted from *Teachings in Prayer Volume One*, T:546 of 14.2.90)

Through the small 'doorway' of death, we encounter God;
and we either praise or shun His glory.
(OIL-S:546)

WITHIN OUR HEARTS.

Many of us are content with the sorts of images we've been given, through the Church, of Heaven, and Heaven's glory; but it's sometimes difficult to imagine what we mean when we declare that God lives 'within' us: within our hearts. Our minds recoil from images of fleshy hearts, or from false unhappy images of our Creator. Perhaps it's easier to look away from ourselves, at someone who is trustworthy, kind, severe and prayerful - and then to say: "I cannot imagine how it 'happens', but I believe that God 'lives' in him."

There's a fire blazing in the human 'heart', in the picture; and that fire represents God's love, active within a person who has said 'Yes' to His presence, and who therefore has made His concerns her own. Each of us is free to welcome God or to reject Him; yet if we live truly united to Christ in faith, hope and love we can be sure of His presence within our souls; and He is present with the Father and the Holy Spirit - One God - Who live within us.

The Three Divine Persons are 'at work' within us. They don't dwell fruitlessly within our hearts and souls. They shed light and blessings upon everyone we 'carry' in our hearts. It's as if They assure each one of us: "If you cherish the whole world in your heart, and if you sincerely welcome Us within your heart, you can be sure that We bless the whole world through your love and generosity."

We ought never to forget the reason, however, why our prayers are always worthwhile, and sometimes delightful. Grace-filled, joyful and effective prayers can be offered from our souls to the Father, in the Spirit, only because of Christ's sacrifice for our sakes on Calvary, and because of our union with Him since our Baptism.

(Text adapted from *Teachings in Prayer Volume One*, T:565 of 10.4.90)

A person full of God's love carries in her heart a
triple fire of love, in which she 'holds' all the needy.
(OIL-S:565)

THE ETERNAL OFFERING.

It's important for us to remember that God the Holy Trinity is one God Who is endless in love, and infinitely great and majestic: united, pure, perfect, simple, and unchanging; and we believe that each of the Three Divine Persons is 'at work' in the Holy Sacrifice of the Mass.

Christ, Who is God-made-man, is Really Present amongst us after the Consecration. He is our High Priest - and also the Victim on our altar; and only through, with and 'in' Christ can we offer perfect praise and homage to the Father, in the Spirit.

Christ proved His love for His Father by loving His Will, even when faithfulness to the mission on which the Father had sent Him led to betrayal, humiliation, desertion, and death on a Cross; and that love, demonstrated on Calvary, is the very love with which the Son loved the Father before the world began. It is also the very love which is being offered by Christ to the Father through the Holy Sacrifice of the Mass, at which the offering of Calvary is re-presented; and it is our privilege to be able to take part in that offering.

At every Mass, we are present at an awesome and holy celebration and commemoration. Even in the darkest church, and amongst sinful or sad people, Christ is present with His holy Angels, in glory.

The 'work' of Christ, and of the Father and the Holy Spirit, is shown in the painting. At every Mass Christ intercedes for His People, from the altar, by offering - at the hands of the priest - His Holy Sacrifice to the Father, in the power of the Holy Spirit.

(Text adapted from *Teachings in Prayer Volume One:* T:572 of 16.4.90)

At every Mass, Christ intercedes for His People,
offering His sacrifice to the Father, in the Spirit.
(OIL-S:572)

HEAVEN TOUCHES EARTH.

A life entirely without Christ - a life with none of His grace or charity - is a life lived in darkness. It's because we've been given new life 'in Christ', and are truly united to Him in everyday life and in worship, that we've been brought into His radiant light; and that light is poured lavishly upon earth from Heaven, through the One Holy Catholic Church which Christ has established and which He guides today, as in past ages, through His Holy Spirit.

To believe this is not to deny that we can learn from other people or develop new approaches in prayer. Good things can be found in other faiths. Self-less and loving persons can be found in all races and places; and yet it was only Christ Who opened up the Way to Heaven by His death on the Cross; and that work of the Cross - Christ's Paschal work - is made effective in our lives through our participation in the Sacred Liturgy. Christ is at work in each of sacraments which He has given to His Church; and during the Holy Eucharist, which is both sacrament and sacrifice, we pray through, with and 'in' Christ, in the great sacrificial prayer which is both holy and effective.

In the painting, we can see that Heaven touches Earth, through Christ's Real Presence in the Mass, and through His intercession from amongst us. It's as though a great light shines around us - a Divine radiance. There's a power at work in the Sacred Liturgy that is greater than any earthly power: stronger than the earthly forces which can harm or obliterate; and God's power strengthens, heals and draws together all it touches.

We who have a living faith in God, and who believe that Christ 'is' our praise of the Father, through the power of the Holy Spirit, are full of gratitude at having been made children of God; children who, even now, can have a foretaste of the Heavenly Banquet.

(Text adapted from *Teachings in Prayer Volume One*, T:576 of 21.4.90)

Heaven touches earth, through Christ's Presence
in the Mass, as His radiance surrounds us.
(OIL-S:576)

31

THE SILENCE OF 'UNKNOWING'.

The stages of prayer through which God leads the willing soul are sometimes uncomfortable or painful - or calming, or even rapturous - or merely puzzling; but whatever our prayer is like, it is always worthwhile, as long as it's sincere.

Every time we turn to God in private, in sincere prayer, as we open our hearts to Him to reveal our fears and hopes and joys, we grow closer to Him, and enable ourselves to participate with ever greater sincerity and understanding in the Holy Mysteries of the Church.

The reverse is true, as well. Every time we participate with renewed love, contrition and fervour in the Sacred Liturgy of the Church, we make more likely our greater progress in private prayer.

Then at last we begin to enter - at God's invitation - the dark, wordless prayer of contemplation. We might experience it, at first, as a terrible lostness in Nothingness, or perhaps as an awesome meeting with an invisible Other Whom our hearts yearn to know whilst still dreading a closer encounter. Or one day, perhaps, our spirit seems to soar in silence into 'Unknowing'.

In such a prayer, the unseen Christ can work His holy work within our soul, in Eternity's silence; and even when our mind is cluttered with distractions, we can pray sincerely and well.

As the picture shows, it's as though a person's mind feebly encircles 'below' the heights, on such occasions; yet her spirit has risen high, into the silence of the Most Holy Trinity, to join with the pure, eternal 'prayer' which is the self-offering, in love, between the Father, the Son and the Holy Spirit.

(Text adapted from *Teachings in Prayer Volume One:* T:588 of 12.5.90)

Even if someone's mind is distracted, her spirit can
rise up to the peace of Eternity, at God's heart.
(OIL-S:588)

33

"IN THE UNITY OF THE HOLY SPIRIT ..."

We rely on Christ to lead us towards the Father in private prayer - as the Holy Spirit is at work in our souls, leading us from darkness to glory, from Nothingness to Presence, or from hiddenness to heights of union; and we also rely on Christ, in liturgical prayer.

Christ is powerfully 'at work' in all seven sacraments of His Church; yet in the greatest of all the sacraments - the Holy Eucharist, also known as the Holy Sacrifice of the Mass - Christ is not only 'at work'. He is Really Present amongst us: Body, Blood, soul and Divinity - though under the appearance of bread and wine; and so we can renew our trust in His powerful intercession on our behalf.

As our priest offers from the altar Christ's one, perfect, saving sacrifice, it's as though Christ - Really Present in our sanctuary - gazes up to the Father in Heaven; and, as is shown in the picture, Christ's hands are outstretched in prayer, as the priest who represents Him reverently shows the Sacred Host to the people present.

Soon afterwards, the priest says to the Father, of Christ: "Through Him, with Him, in Him, in the unity of the Holy Spirit, all glory and honour is Yours, almighty Father, for ever and ever."

And as he speaks, the flames of love - of the burning love which is the Holy Spirit - burn brightly around Christ in the 'fire' of His fervent and loving sacrifice.

(Text adapted from *Teachings in Prayer Volume One,* T:811 of 26.1.91)

We need Christ; and we pray "through him, with him,
and in him, in the unity of the Holy Spirit."
(OIL-S:811)

35

CHRIST WELCOMES THE WILLING SOUL.

Christ is God-made-man; and He really died on the Cross then rose from the grave to new life. He can never die again. He is now in Heaven, where - as is shown in the picture - He holds out His wounded hand to welcome us, as if to show us a 'souvenir' of His great act of love for us: His death on Calvary. He endured torment on earth because of His longing to save us; and He is eternally the High Priest and Mediator for His earthly brothers and sisters. We are very precious to Him. In the depths of our prayer, and even in the apparent tragedy of the moment of our death, Christ welcomes us, His true friends, to the heart of the Holy Trinity.

Consider the wonder of the life to which we are called. The holy and majestic Father, Who eternally embraces His Divine Son and the Holy Spirit, sees and knows everything which exists through Him, and sees and knows everyone He has created. He calls all people towards Himself, to live in His love. The Divine Son, Jesus Christ, once born on earth as true man, and then crucified, is now glorious in Heaven; and everyone who, through union with Christ, 'finds' the Father and lives in Him has left behind a life of darkness and has entered God's holy light. The Holy Spirit - Divine love and eternal source of joy - is endlessly loving the happy souls whom He has been drawing towards the Godhead. He now holds them in His tender embrace for evermore, all their sufferings ended.

It is through faith, repentance, humility and love that we can draw closer to Heaven. We can draw closer to the Father, the Son and the Holy Spirit - Who are One Lord yet Most Holy Trinity: living in ever-lasting light, joy and perfection. Christ said: 'I did not come to call the virtuous, but sinners' (Mt 9:13); so we can approach Him just as we are. We can turn to God in every trial or failure. It is not the self-satisfied who find Him, but those who believe in Him and are sorry for their sins, and who are willing to turn to Him in order to live according to His Will.

(Text adapted from *Teachings in Prayer Volume One*, T:1039C of 16.12.91)

Christ invites us all to share His life, and
welcomes all humble and contrite souls.
(OIL-S:1039C)

37

OUT FROM THE FATHER'S HEART.

The joys of Heaven are no fantasy held out as a means of pacifying weary or rebellious people. They are a continuation and an 'expansion', to an astonishing degree, of the joys which have already been tasted on earth by those who have surrendered their lives to God, not in fear but in love. No earthly joy can compare with the joy, peace and bliss which are found in Heaven. The Father is infinitely good; yet He is also powerful and majestic and beautiful. He is like a vast and infinitely holy fire of love into which we can be led, by the Spirit, through our life in Christ, to experience the love and fulfilment for which we have been yearning.

Christ shares the Father's Divine nature; and Christ is so loving and generous that He longs to save us. It's as if He came out, at His Incarnation, from the 'heart' of the Father, to bring us hope and salvation, rather as a man might soar out from the brilliance of a huge planet in order to rescue small creatures who are lost in Space. We can picture Christ as having come 'outwards' from the Father in order to reach us, and to reach many more persons who are far away, and in danger. At our consent, Christ takes hold of us, and draws us back into the Divine embrace.

It's because Christ is both God and man that He can reconcile us - men, women and children - with our Creator; and our hearts should be ever-thankful that we are being drawn into eternal life and joy through our Baptism, and through many wonderful actions of the Holy Spirit, much of Whose work is secret.

The grace of Christ flows vigorously into our hearts through our trust in Him, and through our moments of sincere and reverent prayer. Through our reception of the Sacred Host - Christ Himself - in Holy Communion we allow our souls to be drawn into His own communion with the Father in the bliss of the Spirit. Christ's grace is then at work in our souls in power and glory.

(Text adapted from *Teachings in Prayer Volume One*, T:1197 of 9.10.92)

Christ came out from the Father's heart,
to draw us back into His embrace.
(OIL-S:1197)

DIVINE LIGHT, EMBODIED.

The marvel of the Christian Faith is that we need no longer rely on our limited observations - about the world and its creatures, and about the Universe with its laws, and its beauty - to know what God is 'like'. From love, He has revealed Himself to Mankind, most fully through His own Son, Jesus Christ, in Whom is 'the fullness of divinity' (Col 2:9). In this way, we have been given overwhelming confirmation that the Father's love is warm, over-flowing, generous and tender. He is always longing to pour out His gifts upon His children on earth.

From His perpetual newness and youth and beauty the Father gives us good things, good news, and spiritual joy: gifts which delight us; and the greatest gift has been our friendship with Christ our Redeemer and His Holy Mother Mary.

Christ is pictured, opposite, as being like an 'image' beamed down to earth from a window in Heaven. We know that, from the glory of the unseen, almighty Father, Who is pure, mysterious and powerful - a furnace of inextinguishable love - Christ our Lord came out, sharing the same glorious Divine nature. By the power of the Holy Spirit, two thousand years ago, Christ took flesh from Mary. Sharing our human nature, Christ has given 'shape' to Divine light.

No impurity exists in Christ, Who is true God, on fire with Divine love. When we hear Christ speak, we are listening to the eternal Word of the Father. When we see Christ touch and console and heal, we see the Father's love for us all, poured out from the heart of the Godhead. And if we picture the glory of Christ, after His death and Resurrection, we picture the Father's glory, which we shall share one day if we have been changed through Christ's transforming love, and if we have remained faithful to the end.

(Text adapted from *Teachings in Prayer Volume One*, T:1244 of 19.12.92)

In sharing our human nature, Christ, God from God,
has given 'shape' to Divine light.
(OIL-S:1244)

41

THE THREE-FOLD EMBRACE.

Day after day, in His Church, Christ is at work to help, comfort and sustain us. It's as if He sends us out into daily life 'fuelled' by the love and the strength which we have received from Him in the sacraments; and we have many other sources of strength and consolation in the sacramentals and blessings, and customs and devotions which we find within the Church - so many of which we take for granted.

By our reverent use of sacraments and sacramentals we receive a marvellous increase of grace in our souls, just as we do whenever we praise God, help a neighbour, curb a selfish instinct, repent of our sins, visit a shrine, pray for a departed soul, defend the Catholic Faith, speak with gratitude about Christ and His Church, or assist our priests: 'other Christs' amongst us. There is no limit to the ways in which we can please God and open our hearts to His graces; yet there are ways He has chosen by which we can be especially confident of receiving His help.

He helps us most surely through the sacraments. He also helps us through every blessing given by the Clergy. When our priest blesses us in the name of the Holy Trinity, it's as if we are wonderfully embraced by God. The priest blesses us in the Name of the Father and of the Son and of the Holy Spirit; and so we can be sure that God is at work.

As indicated in the picture, its as though the Father pours His Heavenly light upon us, through the priest, in each blessing, whilst Christ the Son of God accompanies our soul in the friendship of a spiritual Communion; and - at the very same time - the Holy Spirit is guiding, elevating and comforting our heart.

(Text adapted from *Teachings in Prayer Volume One*, T:1259 of 14.1.93)

*Christ loves to help, console and sustain us through
the sacraments and sacramentals of His Church.
(OIL-S:1259)*

STRIPPED OF ALL GLORY.

We can read in Holy Scripture: 'When peaceful silence lay over all, and night had run the half of her swift course, down from the Heavens, from the royal throne, leapt your all-powerful Word' (Ws 18: 14-15). Every blessing we receive through the Church today, and every sacrament and every word of wisdom, comes to us because Christ our God once lived on earth, and died for us, because He loves us. It was as if He was carried on a wave of Divine grace and power - the power of the Holy Spirit - as He came out from the Father's 'heart', leapt through the 'bars of Heaven', and left behind His glory to live on earth amongst people like ourselves.

Christ is a Divine Person of immense majesty, now united with frail humanity by the extraordinary union of His Divine and human natures. Since the time when He became incarnate in the womb of the Blessed Virgin Mary, He has possessed a real human nature whilst possessing, as ever, the fullness of Divinity. As He grew to maturity in Nazareth, He wasn't someone partly Divine and partly human; nor was He a Divine Person merely disguised as a man; nor was He a man who was 'only' human yet who was like the prophets, though greater than any of them and wholly 'open' to Divine influence. The Church teaches us that Christ - in what is called the hypostatic union - is true God and also true man, and shall ever remain so, in Heaven, where He has lived in His glorified body since His Resurrection and Ascension.

What can we do but humble ourselves before someone as loving as Christ, someone who has come down to us in such intimacy: made the same as us in fragile flesh, and - like each one of us - born of a woman? What a weight and a burden Christ bore in His humanity. What amazing love: that made Him come down to earth so that, side by side with us in our intercessions, but supremely during the Holy Mass, He might call out to the Father on our behalf, praying for help and for salvation.

(Text adapted from *Teachings in Prayer Volume Two*, T:1320 of 6.6.93)

*The Father's 'all-powerful Word' leapt down
from Heaven to earth, at Christ's Incarnation.
(OIL-S:1320)*

CHRIST'S ASCENSION TO GLORY.

The whole Trinity has been at work, to save us, and is still at work today, gathering us together into one family: as a holy People who have found the sure way to Heaven. Yet the 'way' wasn't opened without sacrifice.

In being made man by the Holy Spirit's power, and in obeying the Father's Will in a sinful world, and acting with charity and compassion throughout His life on earth, and never failing to speak the truth, Christ was bound to suffer. He was mocked, deserted, betrayed and tortured by sinful people like ourselves; yet by His patient endurance and His prayers for sinners, He was making up for the disobedience and rebellion of the whole of Mankind. He was making it possible for everyone who would believe in Him and in His atoning sacrifice to share His Divine life and to become an adopted child of God and an heir to the Kingdom.

We know that many of those who don't recognise Christ's Divinity believe that His life on earth ended, forever, in death; yet faithful Christians believe that His life was a triumph, because of His obedience to the Will of the Father, Who couldn't fail to rescue His Son from death, and Who had already planned Christ's Resurrection and Ascension.

Truly, our faith is a wondrous gift. Through it, we know that by the Father's Will, foreknowledge, plan, consent and justice, Christ suffered and died on the Cross; but then He leapt up to His Father in glory by the power and light of the Holy Spirit; and it's as if Christ now draws in His wake those of us who are willing to recognise Him, to thank Him for what He has endured because of our sins, and to follow in His way to Heaven. He wants to banish, in the end, all our darkness and suffering, and to bring us up high to the glory of Heaven: to the Father's embrace.

(Text adapted from *Teachings in Prayer Volume Two*, T:1351 of 4.9.93)

Whoever believes in Christ, and remains faithful,
can also be raised up, one day, to glory.
(OIL-S:1351C)

PURGATORY, IN EARTHLY LIFE.

Only through true contrition can we follow the way which leads through purification towards perfect union with God; yet so much good is achieved by our being 'scoured' through remorse, penance and spiritual darkness, combined with the sufferings of earthly life, that we can look upon our purification as being a priceless gift. Through it, real peace and trust can grow within our souls; and when we are at peace before the Father, and really trust Him, we pray to Him in Christ's name with increasing confidence and gratitude. We see more and more clearly that all our trials have been worthwhile.

To summarise this process, we can say that when someone repents sincerely, perseveres in prayer, bravely bears the shame of his sinfulness, and prays in the name of Jesus, it's as though - like the person in the picture - he voluntarily approaches God the Father in a state of spiritual nakedness. It's as if he walks towards the Father through the fire of the Father's glory; and yet as he approaches, repenting, his soul 'naked' in that fire, yet strong in the life of Christ, all his sins bursts into flame and then disappear. The fire does not touch his flesh; and when his sins are at last consumed he can stand like a happy child in God's presence.

That joyful soul is so pure that he's like a new-born child: naked, innocent and unashamed; and therefore he is fit to be called a true child of the eternal Kingdom (2P 1:11). At the right time, God the Father can clothe him for the 'wedding' (Mt 22:4) which is life in Heaven, in glory; and so we can understand that some of us are invited to walk through our Purgatory not after death, but in this earthly life, through the purification and transformation which God can achieve in our souls by His power, and our co-operation, first in the torments of prayer, and then in the delights of contemplation and union.

(Text adapted from *Teachings in Prayer Volume Two*, T:1366 of 9.11.93)

*Someone who patiently accepts earthly trials and spiritual
purifications undergoes Purgatory in earthly life.
(OIL-S: 1366)*

49

THREE FLAMES OF LOVE.

A firm and lively faith is necessary if we want to remain faithful to God's Will at every moment of our lives - with a sure hope of finding God in Heaven; and we need a sincere love for God and for our neighbour. Yet we can be confident that our faith, hope and love will continue to increase, whether or not we feel fervent or hopeful or loving, as long as we ask God to increase His grace in us, and provided we avoid evil and persevere in doing good.

Our path won't always be dark and dangerous. The knowledge that we're on a safe road will delight us, as our faith grows stronger; and we'll delight in the gifts with which God adorns those who prove themselves to be His friends. We'll delight in the loving and like-minded companions we meet on the road; and, all the time, we'll be confident that the path we follow leads towards Eternal Life, which we hope to spend with the Most Holy Trinity - in Heaven.

Even during our life on earth we are wrapped in God's love. Even now we are led by Jesus, and we are directed by His Spirit, as we walk towards the Father. As you can see in the painting, it's as if God guides the footsteps of each one of us, on our long journey, so that each willing soul can step into the centre of a great light which stretches across the pathway; and the single great light consists of three huge flames which rise up to enfold the frail traveller. Intertwined, those flames hold her within their warm and peaceful embrace.

At every instant, we live at the heart of the Holy Three - One God - Who almost carry us, it seems, as we walk towards Heaven. The Three Divine Persons are like three great flames of love; yet They are one fire, in Whose unchanging light we already live, even before we reach Heaven's perfection.

(Text adapted from *Teachings in Prayer Volume Two*, T:1385 of 1.1.94)

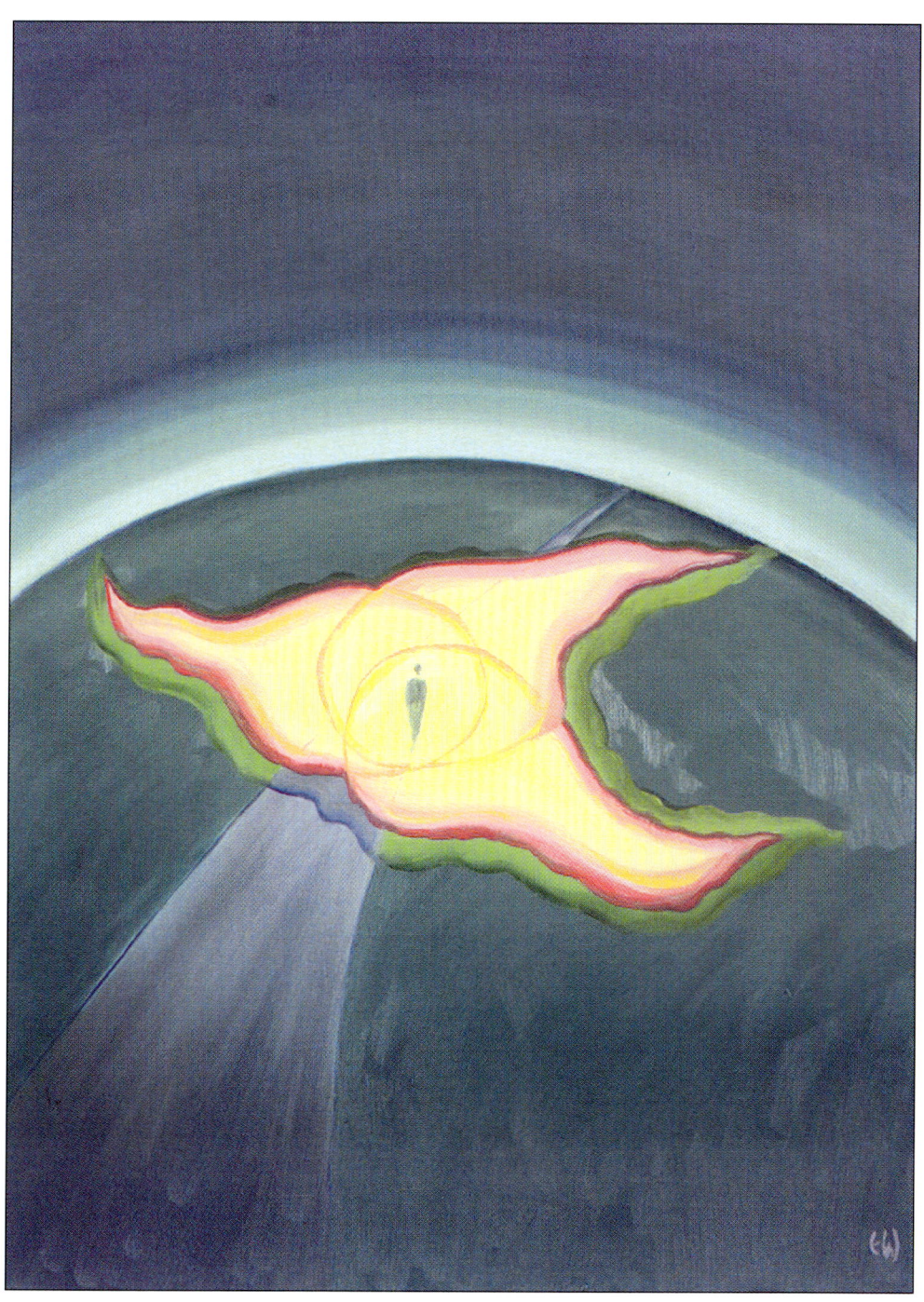

*During life on earth, God's children are led, directed
and enfolded within three great flames of love.
(OIL-S:1385A)*

THREE DIVINE PERSONS: ONE FIRE.

To live by faith is to be content to believe in things we can't yet touch, to trust in Persons we can't yet see, and to develop in ways which aren't yet evident to us; yet wonderful things are happening in our souls and lives if we try to give up sin, imitate Christ in His obedience to the Father's Will, live for love, and try to fulfil our vocation.

Almighty God - the Holy Trinity - lives within our souls. We need to pause, to consider the wonder of our life of union and communion. How astonishing it is, that weak creatures are loved, held, and guided, in a personal and enduring relationship, by the great Lord and Creator Who made the Universe and everything in it.

Truly, if we have wholly entrusted ourselves to God, and are reconciled, we now share in God's life: the life of the Father Who waits before us, the life of Jesus our Lord and daily Companion, and the life of the Holy Spirit Who leads us onwards; and we have learned that none of the Three Divine Persons lacks anything, yet none is ever 'without' the Others; and we fortunate souls are embraced by Three Divine Persons, yet held within the unity of the Godhead. We have been created by and are now cherished by a Triune love.

Each perfect and Divine Person Who reaches out to console us, in the picture, can be seen as wholly flame and wholly fire; yet the Three, together, are one flame or one fire in which three 'flames' are distinct yet united. This one fire of love - the Godhead - is simple yet three-fold It is bright, pure, perfect and everlasting: one God, unrivalled, Who is living and true.

(Text adapted from *Teachings in Prayer Volume Two*, T:1385 of 1.1.94)

The Three Divine Persons reach out - like a single flame -
to console a 'child of God'.
(OIL-S:1385B)

A PRECIOUS CHILD.

We are sometimes tempted to imagine that God is 'absent', when the truth is that He is very close indeed, and is lovingly holding us in existence; yet we can increase our faith in Him by making an act of faith each time we begin our prayer. If we say, as we begin: "I believe that You are close to me. I believe that You love me" - we have opened wide the 'door' of our souls; and His spiritual light can shine in, to increase our hope and faith and love.

If we have been made adopted children of God, through Christ, we have a sure hope of Heaven, if we remain faithful to the end; and throughout our journey towards the Kingdom we should remain confident in prayer. Every sincere prayer which we offer through Christ to the Father, in the Spirit, is greeted with delight. The Father delights in the humility with which we approach Him, and in the trust which we demonstrate by our prayers.

Divine Love is pictured, opposite, as being like the tender embrace of a father for his child. Whenever we pray with real trust and humility we are very close to Heaven's 'border'. It's as though Heaven lies just above our heads: and 'Heaven is our homeland' (Ph 3:20): a place of light and sweetness and love.

It's as though our Heavenly Father, Who is one with the Son and the Spirit, is always waiting at the edge of Heaven: waiting to listen to our prayers. The littlest prayer, and the briefest whisper to God, is welcomed, heard, valued and rewarded. It's as though the Father is lovingly, tenderly, stroking the neck of His own dear child, as He reaches out to caress a precious supplicant who trusts in Him and confides every need.

As God's children, we have the sure knowledge that He loves us at every moment. We can turn to Him whenever we please, in trusting prayer: certain of being heard and answered.

(Based upon *Teachings in Prayer Volume Two*, T:1396 of 21.1.94)

The Father reaches out, tenderly, to caress
a precious soul who trusts in His love.
(OIL-S:1396)

55

A LIVING CONNECTION.

If we're grateful that we've been made children of God we rejoice in the presence of the Holy Spirit within our souls. We honour and adore Him; and we express our gladness that He has led us to a place within the Church, which is Christ's Body on earth.

It is 'in' the Spirit's fire of love that we Christians are united with one another, through prayer. As we pray in the Name of Jesus, in the love of our Heavenly Father, we enter into a deeper and more intimate communion with the Three Persons of the Holy Trinity. We rest at the heart of their Divine life.

If we are close to Christ and to His Holy Mother, and love the Church and treasure the sacraments, we love to be united with one another in the Spirit, with Christ and with the Saints and the Holy Souls: one in praise of the Father, during the Holy Sacrifice of the Mass.

Our prayers arise as one great prayer to the Father: a prayer which is offered with, in and through Christ, in what is a living memorial of Christ's saving work; and the picture illustrates the fact that Christ's prayer from our altar, during the Holy Sacrifice of the Mass, is like an umbilical cord by which the prayers of weak human beings reach Heaven, and by which grace and light are given to those within its reach on Earth.

A powerful, living connection is made with Heaven through Christ, in the Spirit. Since we are God's children we are drawn away from darkness, uncertainty and fear; and we live in hope of seeing the Father of glory when our earthly life has ended.

(Text adapted from *Teachings in Prayer Volume Two*, T:1409 of 2.3.94)

Christ's prayer from our altar is like an umbilical cord,
through which we receive grace and light from Heaven.
(OIL-S:1409)

TWO 'ARMS' FROM THE FATHER.

The greater is our love for the Church, for the Sacred Scriptures, and for the Holy Eucharist, the greater is our delight in pondering the marvellous things which God has done for us. We begin to burn with the desire to share the Good News more widely and more boldly - and to burn with the desire to see God loved. As we grow in faith, we're glad to share what we've learned, to help to deliver other people from hopelessness and isolation and sin.

In the picture, it's as though God the Father is hidden far above, in glory; yet His love for Mankind is so great that He has reached out from on high to send powerful help towards a sinful world. It's as though, through His plan of salvation - through His self-revelation - He has enfolded humanity in an 'embrace of God'.

The Word and the Holy Spirit are like two arms from God the Father. We can remind ourselves, yet again, that the Word took flesh from the Virgin Mary, and lived His earthly life in total love for the Father and for Mankind - and died on a Cross for our sins. After His Resurrection and Ascension to Heaven, Christ sent the Holy Spirit to the hearts of His followers; and that same Spirit still guides Christ's Church today - and is at work in other hearts which don't yet recognise Him; so we can say that all who live on earth are touched by the powerful and loving actions of the Most Holy Trinity: Father, Son and Holy Spirit - one holy Creator.

For century upon century the living God has been calling out to us all, urging us to come out of darkness, and to enter His glorious light.

(Text adapted from *Teachings in Prayer Volume Two*, T:1439 of 28.5.94)

The Father of glory has sent out to us His Son and
His Spirit: like two arms to embrace the world.
(OIL-S:1439)

THE PATTERN OF OUR LIFE.

Whatever sort of life we lead, Christ's powerful help is ours, as we struggle against temptations.

The person in the painting is looking upwards in prayer, as if she can see Christ standing at the 'edge' of Heaven. He cannot leave us alone, even if we sometimes imagine that He is far away from us. Only the thinnest of 'veils' hides Him from our sight.

Christ's whole desire is to reach out to us, draw us into His light, and draw us towards the invisible Father, as the Holy Spirit guides us in the freely-made acts and efforts by which we reach out to Christ in daily life.

The Holy Trinity is powerfully at work in our lives: at work in our soul, and in our everyday life, when we love God wholeheartedly and share in His life, and co-operate with His Will and actions. As we pray to the Father, we can be sure that the Word of God - Jesus Christ, Who loves us - is drawing us up to the heart of the Father; and the Holy Spirit 'presents' us to Him as a holy offering.

This pattern of co-operation with the work of the Holy Trinity should be the pattern of our whole life's work and our whole life's prayer. This 'pattern' is available for everyone who lives in and for God. It consists of the 'interweaving' of all of our prayers, thoughts and actions into God's Divine and unending work of love!

(Text adapted from *Teachings in Prayer Volume Two*, T:1469 of 26.8.94)

*Christ is powerfully at work in our lives, through
the Spirit, to drawn us up to the Father's heart.
(OIL-S:1469A)*

CHRIST AWAITS US.

In times of trial or doubt we might sometimes be tempted to doubt God's love, or to echo the Psalmist who said: 'What is man, that you should spare a thought for him?' (Ps 8:4).

Perhaps we begin to wonder once again how the Lord, the all-holy, can be concerned with 'little ones' like ourselves: with weak people who find it hard to do good.

We even hear in the words of the Mass that God has "no need of our praise", since nothing we might say can cause or augment the infinite, perpetual bliss which is of the essence of the life of the Holy Trinity, in Eternity. Yet we should never doubt that our praises are worthwhile. It is our duty to honour God. Our hearts and minds were made for worship; and so we are fulfilled and helped to some degree whenever we pray.

Our praise is also worthwhile because - as you see in the painting - Christ our Lord is at the heart of the Godhead. He is true man as well as true God, and He is now at the heart of Heaven; and since we are His true brothers and sisters, we touch His heart very deeply by our loving praises.

Christ is made happy by our veneration, and by our praise of the Father: praise which we offer through Christ, in the Holy Spirit. Christ awaits us, at the heart of Heaven's triple glory; and His heart longs for us to join Him. This is His plan for Mankind; this is what would cause Him tremendous delight: to see a great crowd of the Faithful loving Him and longing to meet Him; to see us all pouring like a river into the Godhead, into the heart of the Most Holy Trinity.

(Text adapted from *Teachings in Prayer Volume Two*, T:1476 of 17.9.94)

Christ, at the 'heart' of the Godhead, longs
to see us enter Heaven, to join Him.
(OIL-S:1476)

EVERY KNEE SHALL BOW.

We know little about Heaven; yet we know enough - through the words of Christ, and the words of His saintly followers - to be certain that all who enjoy Heaven, enjoy freedom from sin and pain. Perfect fulfilment is theirs at last, in God's love and light and glory; and they are united in love and praise, in a way we can't imagine, with the whole Church of earth and Heaven and Purgatory.

The Three Divine Persons - one God - Who are now reigning in the blazing light of glory are eternally adored in Heaven; and it's encouraging for us to remember that whenever we pray fervent prayers upon earth, our prayers are united to the prayers of the Saints and Angels who are gathered in thousands around the Throne of the Godhead. All who pray to God 'in Christ' enjoy a true 'communion' with the Saints in Heaven. The Saints look with joy and wonder upon every trustful soul who approaches the Father with reverence and love and offers prayers in the Name of Jesus.

The picture serves as a reminder that whenever we turn our hearts towards Heaven, we address the Holy Trinity: three Divine Persons Who are too glorious to see, yet each of Whom is crowned with majesty. We've heard in Holy Scripture: 'Before me, every knee shall bow' (Is 45:23); and here, where a little figure kneels in loving reverence, the Father's fatherhood is symbolised by a triple crown, like that which belongs to the Holy Father, the Pope; and the Son of God is crowned - as is the Holy Spirit, also - with a halo which signifies His holiness; and whoever comes very close to God in prayer is bathed in the light of Heaven, and shares in Heaven's joy. Joy, radiance and wisdom and peace belong to the state of life which is achieved by those who are led to the heart of the Holy Trinity, through prayer. Only through God's grace do souls endure His burning touch. Only by His grace can anyone bring to others the knowledge of His love, and beauty, and power and glory.

(Text adapted from *Teachings in Prayer Volume Two:* T:1508 of 29.11.94 and T:1541 of 27.1.95)

Only by God's grace can we hope to meet God
in His love, beauty, power and glory.
(OIL-S:1541)

A 'CIRCLE' OF PRAISE.

The three Divine Persons are at work in every 'Christian' prayer. If we kneel in prayer before the tabernacle, and look towards Christ our Saviour Who is Really Present, it's as though there is a fiery movement around us, like a wind or a flame: a fiery 'circle' of prayer which is in motion for as long as we continue in worship and petition.

This is shown out in the painting, where someone prays before the sanctuary. From Heaven, above, the Father has sent down His loving Spirit, to enable that person to pray; and when she does so, in response to the Spirit's touch, she pours out the Spirit's own fierce, Divine love towards Christ Who is Present in the tabernacle; and it's as if Christ 'catches' that fiery Breath and hurls it up to His Father, thus hurling love, in a fiery arc, up towards Heaven where it 'began'; and thus Christ, Who is always praising His Father - and Who praises Him on our behalf - sends to the Father a Divine prayer of delight: of praise, thanks, reparation and intercession; and into His prayer, Christ weaves - as we kneel before Him - our praise, with our thanks, our reparation and petitions. Thus is completed the fiery and fervent 'circle' of praise which is the prayer of the Holy Trinity, a prayer in which we are included because of our 'life-in-Christ', our faith - as we pray 'in the Holy Spirit' (Jude 1:20) - and our open-hearted longing to praise the Father with and through Christ our Lord.

What a marvel it is, that we can take part in God's own, holy prayer. The 'circle' of God's prayer on earth - as He acts through and within our souls - is like His glorious prayer in Heaven, which is pure and perpetual, without end or beginning. It is the work of three Divine and holy Persons, in the united and loving communion of the Father, the Son, and the Holy Spirit.

(Text adapted from *Teachings in Prayer Volume Two*, T:1548 of 4.2.95)

The Father sends the Holy Spirit to a soul, to make
her one with Christ, in praise of the Father.
(OIL-S:1548)

AT HEAVEN'S DOOR.

Even now, day by day, with thousands of our spiritual brothers and sisters upon Earth, we are being drawn closer to Heaven; yet it's only through the work of salvation which Christ, long ago, accomplished on earth that we can live in hope of reaching Heaven; and so the Church thanks Him for what He has done for us all through His Passion, Death and Resurrection, and also for His Ascension into Heaven. That is one of the events which we commemorate in every Mass, and celebrate annually with special joy.

The picture opposite conveys the truth that Christ's work on earth was successful. It's as though the Father in Heaven opens Heaven's door, to greet His risen, ascended Son; and as Christ looks at the face of His Father He draws His attention to the many thousands of His earthly brothers and sisters who are going to be brought on high by the Spirit's power. Christ's followers know that humanity is their bond with Christ, and that Christ's saving work on earth is their cause for hope, and that their faith in Christ is soon to be rewarded. Only because of Him has the 'door' to Heaven opened.

If we are true followers today, then Christ has a message for us to share. He is longing to save us. He is longing to see us, His real brothers and sisters, enter the glory which He now enjoys.

Only because of His return to the Father - making a Way, opening a pathway - has Christ given hope to us who love Him: to us who shelter beneath His outstretched arm: to us who cling to this God-Man, Who died to save us. Only those who know Him and who follow Him - our Divine Saviour yet real brother - can walk the pathway to Heaven: the pathway which was made ready through His Passion and His triumph.

(Text adapted from *Teachings in Prayer Volume Two*, T:1588 of 25.5.95)

By His saving work, and the Spirit's power, Christ can bring
us to the door of Heaven, where the Father awaits us.
(OIL-S:1588)

EVERLASTING LIFE.

The Three Divine Persons are eternally unchanging, and yet they are eternally 'at work', to sanctify and guide us; and the work and unity of the three Divine Persons in the one God is best described by a symbol; and an apt symbol by which to express the Mystery which is God's Trinity-in-Unity, is what is called a "Russian wedding ring". We can picture a wedding ring which consists of three shining bands of metal, each of which is a circle, but a circle which apparently twists one way and then another to accommodate the 'movements' of the two other metallic circles which are intertwined around it and with each other.

How simple is such a ring, and how beautiful! No band is larger than another. None has a beginning or an end. Each is perfect in its own shape and its own beauty. None gains anything by being with the others, since the three together are a ring just as the single band is a ring; yet if we imagine the three bands flowing over and around and next to one another smoothly, unceasingly, and slowly - in a steady manner - in eternity, we have a picture in mind which symbolises God's Trinity-in-Unity: God's inner life, of which He has revealed something to us, through Christ. It is a life in which three Divine Persons, one God, exist as beautiful and changeless, and yet are 'at work' unceasingly, 'flowing' in the heart of eternity.

The small jewels which are shining upon the ring in the illustration represent the moments of wisdom which God shares with certain privileged souls in contemplative prayer. Such bursts of knowledge are like sparks which glisten upon the brilliant 'river' which is God's Divine light and life as it 'flows' ever-lastingly within the Godhead. They are like minuscule glints thrown out from the torrent of God's burning glory. No such 'spark' does more than reflect the merest scrap of God's radiance; yet each one conveys a little of His infinite wisdom, so causing the soul to praise God with greater fervour and to burn with the longing to see God in Heaven.

(Adapted from *Teachings in Prayer Volume Two*, T:1626 of 26.7.95)

A triple wedding ring is a symbol of the Godhead:
of three Persons yet one God.
(OIL-S:1626)

A FLAMING ARROW OF FIRE.

We receive an increase of Divine life within our souls whenever we welcome Christ in the Holy Eucharist. He can bring us glory, bliss and light; yet He doesn't come to us alone when He comes to us in Holy Communion, since wherever He works and acts His Father and the Holy Spirit also work and act. Christ doesn't go 'outside' the Godhead in order to reach a soul on earth. No-one and nothing can separate the Persons of the Holy and undivided Trinity.

Whenever Christ is Present within our souls in a sacramental manner we can be certain that He has come to us with His love, and with the Spirit's power and the Father's life.

We can look upon Christ's fervent 'descent' to our heart, in Holy Communion, as being like the descent from Heaven of a great striated flame of love, like an arrow. The 'arrow' which falls so swiftly towards us represents the work and action of the Holy Trinity at the time when we receive Christ in the Blessed Sacrament. God is powerfully at work in our souls, through Christ's sacramental Presence; and we mustn't imagine that His grace in us is fruitless.

Without Christ we can do nothing (Jn 15:5). He has said this. Yet we can be confident that He can help and change us whenever we turn to Him in Holy Communion, or in daily prayer, or in adoration before Him in the Blessed Sacrament - whether in an empty church or during Exposition. His Presence is glorious. 'In' Him, in the sanctuary - and in our souls in Holy Communion - is found the fullness of the light and glory of the Godhead. We must believe that He is powerful enough to help us in every fear or danger. Nothing can defeat Him; and if we cling to Him, trusting in Him, nothing shall 'defeat' us.

(Text adapted from *Teachings in Prayer Volume Two*, T:1632 of 29.7.95)

The love of God pierces our hearts, in Holy Communion, as
Christ comes to us with the Father and the Holy Spirit.
(OIL-S: 1632)

TOUCHING HEAVEN.

As we pray before the altar during the Mass we are closely united with everyone else who offers the Holy Sacrifice with us, when Christ is Really Present amongst us in sacramental form, and when His Holy Sacrifice is offered to the Father at the hands of our priest.

In the painting, it's as though, through His Real Presence amongst us, Christ is standing at the top of a high mountain; and as He holds up His right hand to His Heavenly Father - Who is reaching down towards Him - Christ is surrounded by those friends, ourselves included, who are united in one effort to 'touch' Heaven, through His intercession; and this mountain is completely obscured by the crush of fervent people who are holding firmly onto one another and onto Christ. So the Holy Sacrifice of the Mass is offered through Christ; yet it is a collective act of worship in which all sorts of benefits are rightly sought by the participants, and through which Glory is given to the Father.

Through our participation in the Holy Mass we benefit not only ourselves, but all of the people in our hearts whom we love so dearly. Whenever we pray with our spiritual brothers and sisters, united in one intention - which is to offer reverent and loving prayer through Christ our Mediator, to the Father, in the Spirit - it's as if we are 'touching' Heaven. It's as though we are all bound together, with Christ, in a single Body; and our prayer is successful. Through the merits of Christ's Sacrifice, we are truly in touch with the Father. In this one great prayer Christ is pleading in our midst for all that will make us most joyful eternally. As we reach up to Heaven, united with Christ in prayer, we can be sure that we are lifting up our beloved friends and relations to our Heavenly Father. How can they fail to benefit, when we 'carry' them in our hearts, and pray sincere prayers for them in Christ's Presence?

(Text adapted from *Teachings in Prayer Volume Two*, T:1685 of 13.10.95)

We 'touch' Heaven whenever we gather together at Mass,
to offer praise through Christ to the Father, in the Spirit.
(OIL-S:1685A)

GAZING UPON THE WORLD.

We can invoke and honour the Most Holy Trinity in a hundred different ways: for example, when we bless ourselves by using holy water as we enter a church, or when we say: "Glory be to the Father, and to the Son, and to the Holy Spirit", as we pray the Rosary, perhaps, or at the end of a Psalm, or when we've said grace before a meal, or at the end of every episode of private prayer; and since the Holy Trinity holds frail creatures such as ourselves, and the whole Universe, in existence, we are right to offer perpetual homage and thanks and love.

What security and joy we can have, knowing that the three Divine Persons - One God - are endlessly loving, united and patient. We can picture the Godhead as being like a circle of light which is hovering far above us. It's as if the three loving Persons are gazing upon the world, upon its millions of busy people; and They are asking: "How many are loving Us at this moment?" How terrible it is, that so many of us have ignored our God and Creator, or even disbelieved in His existence.

If we think about our attitude to God we can ask: "How many of us are following God's wishes by living as His true disciples?" Whoever is truly devoted to Christ is wholehearted in love for Him, fervent in prayer, and is eager to learn from Christ's teachers: from the Holy Father and the other Bishops. A true disciple is grateful for gifts, lavish with his time and his service, delighted by His Heavenly Food, and faithful in interceding for the Church: for Christ's own People; and sincere followers of Christ do all they can to encourage one another to be faithful, not disobedient.

(Text adapted from *Teachings in Prayer Volume Two* T:1720 of 28.11.95)

God the Holy Trinity gazes upon the earth, as millions of busy people
ignore their Creator, or disbelieve in His existence.
(OIL-S:1704)

FROM A BRIGHT CLOUD.

Every true Christian rejoices in the knowledge that Christ our God came 'out' from the God the Father to join us in our earthly life; and it's because Christ's nature is two-fold, since His Incarnation, that He provides a marvellous link between Mankind and the Godhead.

The picture represents the powerful way in which Christ can help frail human beings. The bright cloud represents the Divine nature which Christ shares with the Father; and that cloud has changed shape at one end, where it has grown longer, and has become man-shaped. That 'area' represents Christ; and He is seen almost touching the earth's surface. It is because Christ is truly human that He is holding tightly to a circle of people who have accepted His invitation to reach out and cling to Him; yet it's because Christ shares the Divine nature of the Father that Christ can share His Divine life with His earthly friends and draw them up towards the heart of the Godhead; and He does so through the power of the Holy Spirit.

When Christ took a human nature his Divine nature remained always His, because He is a Divine Person; so it was quite impossible that He should not have been lifted up and drawn back into the Father's embrace at the end of His earthly life; and the Good News for us is that if we are united to Christ, and are indwelt by His Spirit, we have a sure hope of sharing in His Resurrection.

It's important for us to remember that Christ isn't at work alone. The Three Divine Persons - one God - are powerfully at work to sanctify and save us; and They are powerfully at work in our private prayer as well as in the Sacred Liturgy, as they urge us to be loving and faithful and hopeful.

(Text adapted from *Teachings in Prayer Volume Three*, T:1776 of 15.1.96)

From the 'bright cloud' of the Divinity, Christ came out,
to share our human nature and to rescue us.
(OIL-S:1776A)

WORKING AS ONE.

Since God's whole desire and plan for us is to draw us into the heart of the Godhead - at our consent - we're surely wise if we seize every opportunity of learning more about Him, and of fulfilling His Will for us: His plan. Whoever longs to be more surely established in the very heart of God can also resolve to approach God in prayer with even greater love and trust and reverence; yet he can also ask for the grace to be made more compassionate towards his neighbour. By our prayers for other people, for example, we not only help other people; we allow God to draw us more surely into His life, that is, into the life of the Three Divine Persons: one God - as shown in the painting. The 'whole' Trinity is at work during our every prayer.

For example, if we ask for the guidance of the Holy Spirit and are taught by God our Father, Christ is not absent. Indeed, in our loving union with the Holy Trinity we are 'held' in Christ's embrace, we are 'turned' towards the Father who dwells above; and we are united with the Father by the love of the Holy Spirit to Whom we turned, initially, for help, and Who now welcomes us and makes us joyful.

An adopted 'child of God' who has been purified, transformed and closely united to God can enjoy a true participation in His life. Through His free gift, and His infinite generosity, God gives such a soul a real share in His Divine nature. In such a union, when that happy soul enters the prayer of unknowing, he tastes God's own perpetual bliss. When that soul is one with God, through prayer, he shares in God's Self-knowledge. When he sees the state of his own soul, and recognises his own intentions, he shares God's insight. When he is Christ-like in his acts and thoughts and prayers he acts with God's love. When his self-surrender to God is fruitful, he shares in God's creative power; and when, for love of God, and to help his neighbour, he unites each of his loving sacrifices with that made by Christ, the Crucified, he shows out God's love and compassion.

(Text adapted from *Teachings in Prayer Volume Three*, T:1794 of 30.1.96 and T:1704 of 03.11.95)

The Three Divine Persons are at work in our
prayer, holding us in Their embrace.
(OIL-S:1794)

81

OVERSHADOWING THE ALTAR.

What a marvellous truth it is: that the Holy Trinity is at work not only in individual souls and in the events of the world, but also in our sanctuary, in our Eucharistic celebration.

Our priest stands at the altar, and obeys Christ today by doing what Christ did at His 'Last Supper.' The priest offers thanks to God the Father for all His gifts, but especially for the gifts of bread and wine which have been brought to the altar; and then our priest prays in the name of Christ our Lord, to ask: "Send your Holy Spirit" - to consecrate the bread and wine; and this is a powerful prayer, which is swiftly answered at the Consecration.

In the image, it seems as though a great veil is moving across the sanctuary; and yet that 'veil' is a powerful force, and a movement. It is like an arm reaching down from Heaven, or like a gigantic wing, the tip of which brushes the holy altar.

A great power is at work in the Consecration: Divine power. By a mere 'touch', the Holy Spirit - almighty God - changes the inanimate substances of bread and wine into the Sacred Body and Blood of Christ our Saviour. All who are present should pray with great reverence as the Holy Spirit overshadows the altar to bring about this marvel, by which Christ is made really Present amongst us in what we call a sacramental manner. He is with us 'whole and entire': His body, blood, soul and Divinity. Truly, He is the 'living bread which has come down from Heaven' (Jn 6:51) - through the Father's love and the work of the Holy Spirit.

(Text based upon *Teachings in Prayer Volume Three*, T:1839 of 15.3.96)

Divine power is at work at the Consecration,
as the Holy Spirit overshadows the altar.
(OIL-S:1839)

83

DISTINCT BUT UNITED.

The painting is of a fire, which represents something of the marvellous life and 'work' of the Holy Trinity. The image is of a living fire which is composed of three great flames: each of which is distinct; yet the three make one flame, or one light, which represents the Godhead.

Each flame appears to be different from the others, as we watch their flickering movements; yet these differences represent not the Divine Persons but rather the works which are attributed to different Divine Persons: what we call their appropriations. We notice, too, that each flame is the same as the others, though only in the sense of all three possessing the same nature - which, in this illustration, is fire. Each flame, meanwhile is 'overlapping' the others, whilst each one glows brightly. Each entwines itself with the others in peaceful and graceful movements: and this 'entwining' can convey to us the way in which the Three Persons, Who are one God, do in fact act as one.

Wherever the Holy Spirit is at work, the Father and the Son are at work; wherever the Father is at work, He is at work with both the Son and the Holy Spirit; and we know that wherever the Son is at work, the Father and the Holy Spirit, also, are active.

We can think of God as being like a fire which is forever unchanging, calm, inextinguishable, indefinable, and uncontainable: like a fire which has no source. Neither lamp, candle nor tinder caused this fire to shine. This 'fire' - these flames - exists of itself, and represents our God, Who is Three-in-One and Who has neither beginning nor end.

(Text adapted from *Teachings in Prayer Volume Three*, T:1913 of 2.6.96)

God is Three-in-One, as if like three great flames
which are one fire, inextinguishable and glorious.
(OIL-S:1913)

THE LOVING TOUCH OF THE SPIRIT.

God is the powerful and majestic Lord of all things; and He is also love. Love is His nature. To share love is His eternal purpose; and so the Father cannot fail to reward His friends for their struggles to please Him and to be fit for Heaven. He loves to reach out to a contrite heart, from Heaven's splendour, to reveal how great is the height and depth of the loving union which has been brought about between Himself and the soul, through Christ, and through the prayers of the Blessed Virgin Mary - and after that soul's fierce purification.

It is through the loving 'touch' of the Holy Spirit - as if by an outstretched hand, in the picture - that the Father brings light and joy to a soul in prayer, demonstrates His love, shares His life to a greater degree, teaches that soul about His nature, and invites her to rest more frequently with Him, in contemplation: to rest with God, within her own soul, as if within a tabernacle or a tent. Whoever meets God in such a true union and communion has been brought by the Holy Spirit close to the furnace of love which is shining at the heart of Divine life; and that soul begins to fathom God's nature: to glimpse Divine love in its beauty and perfection; and that Divine love consists of gentleness and peace as well as power and glory.

Divine love is the source of all true love, and the cause of true spiritual joy. It is the light which illumines the souls of God's children. It is the blissful burning which wounds the heart of all who love truth, goodness and beauty. It is the sweet love which binds together all true friends. Divine love is unchanging yet alive, warm and effective. It is the treasure which is found by all who enjoy true spousal love in earthly life, yet also the eternal prize of all who put their trust in God, and deny themselves, in His service - and who remain faithful. It is also the fire at the heart of every sort of true, loving communion, whether between frail people in earthly life, or between an individual soul and her Creator.

(Text adapted from *Teachings-in-Prayer Volume Three,* T:1941 of 23.6.96)

The Father brings light and joy to a soul in prayer
by the loving touch of the Holy Spirit.
(OIL-S:1941)

IN RADIANT SPLENDOUR.

We make great progress in the spiritual life when we really know, believe and delight in the knowledge that God is love. From love, God created us. From love, He gradually revealed Himself to His Chosen People, before revealing Himself most fully in Him Who was conceived by the Holy Spirit of the Virgin Mary: Jesus Christ, of Whom St. Paul tells us: "In his body lives the fullness of divinity" (Col 2:9). From love, Christ founded a Church for us to join, giving us the sacraments in which we receive a great out-pouring of His graces. From love, Christ is Really Present in the Blessed Sacrament of His Sacred Body and Blood, and gives Himself to us in Holy Communion. Christ is true God: the very Lord Who spoke with Elijah and with Moses, and the Prophets; that's why we are sometimes so powerfully affected by our union and Communion.

The picture offers a pale reminder that God lives within our souls, in His purity and dazzling splendour, if we are living in a 'state of grace'. Here are Three Persons yet one God; so we must believe not only in Christ's power, and in the Father's power, but also in the almighty power of the Holy Spirit Whom we're not able to 'picture' as easily as we've pictured Jesus or our Heavenly Father, and so perhaps approach with little love or confidence.

The Father loves to hear the prayers we offer in Jesus' name; and Christ loves to hear our trusting prayers; yet we're wise also to turn to the Holy Spirit for help in difficult times. He is true God; and therefore He is Holy, adorable, majestic and infinitely kind; and He is equal to Christ and the Father, in His perfection. By His power, the Holy Spirit can give us what we ask of Him; He can give us purity, courage and peace, as we surrender our lives to Christ once more, in order to reach the Father: yearning to be brought 'safe to his glorious presence, innocent and happy' (Jude 1:24).

(Text adapted from *Teachings in Prayer Volume Three*, T:1978 of 11.8.96)

God the Holy Trinity dwells in purity and splendour
in the souls of His faithful children.
(OIL-S:1978)

NO OTHER WAY.

Our Father in Heaven is utterly delighted by our longing to serve Him well. He is ever-loving: ever-willing to make us worthy of His service and, by the merits of Christ His Son, to make us worthy of entering Heaven. Yet only by Christ's sacrifice on the Cross and through His Divine power, has a way been made in which we can follow: the way illustrated in the painting: the way which had been closed, because of Mankind's sinful disobedience soon after the dawn of man's life on earth. By Christ perfect obedience to the Father's Will, reparation has been made for Mankind's sins; and we are all in Christ's debt: even people who don't yet know about Him, or who refuse to believe in Him.

Christ the God-man was born on earth for this: to love, to heal, to teach and to set an example, but, supremely, to die. He knew that after His death He would rise from the dead, and thus rise up from the darkness of a sinful world to pierce Heaven's light; and He succeeded. He has made it possible for us to follow: to soar swiftly through the narrow way which opens out into the breadth of Heaven's light, and so to reach the Father.

Christ has told us that there is no other way into Heaven but His way: a way made by Him at His Resurrection when He returned in glory to the Father; yet Christ's way is now open to all who believe in Him and have been baptised into His life: people who, in order to live a new life in Him and to keep His commandments, feed on Him in the Holy Eucharist and welcome the presence of His Holy Spirit into their hearts and lives. It's through Christ's merits, therefore, that we speak with confidence to our Heavenly Father, rely on Christ's help in intercession, stand beside Christ in prayer, and offer Christ's Precious Blood, as our gift. We must live in hope that since we love Christ we'll rise upwards, one day, like Him: clothed in white, as if in the 'wedding garment' which Christ described as being the suitable clothing for the King's banquet (Mt 22:11).

(Text adapted from *Teachings in Prayer Volume Three,* T:2003 of 7.9.96)

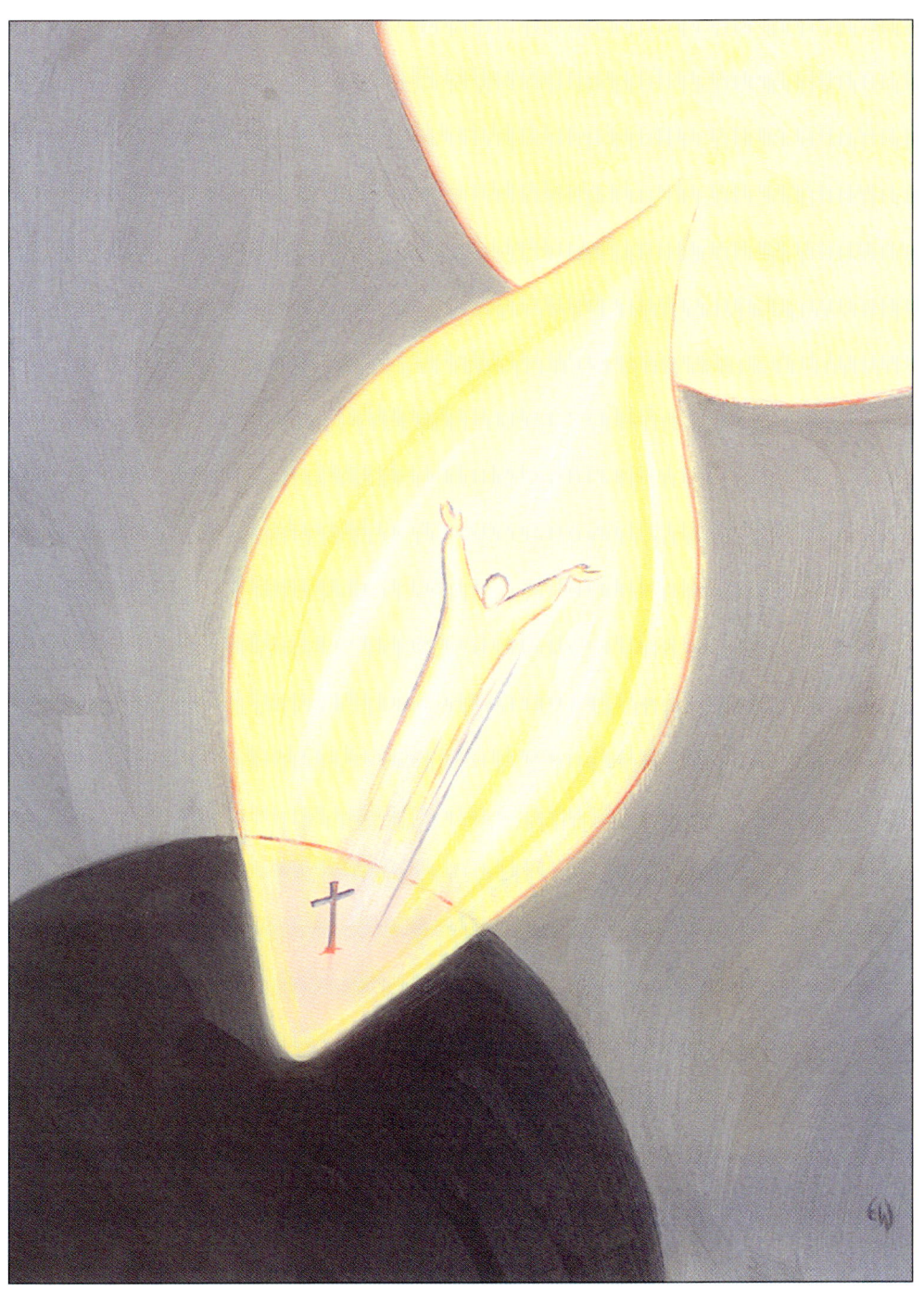

*Only by Christ's sacrifice of Himself on the Cross
has a way been made to Heaven: the only way.
(OIL-S:2003B)*

DIVINE GLORY, IN THE SANCTUARY.

The Holy Eucharist is at the very heart and centre of Catholic life. It is the 'Source and summit of the Christian Life' (CCC: 1324); and all who treasure the gifts with which the Church showers us love to go to Exposition and Benediction in order to prolong or to offer thanks for the joy which we have found through Christ's Eucharistic Presence in the Mass. Even if we are blind to Heaven's light, for the moment, it shines before us as we adore Christ in the Blessed Sacrament of the altar. 'In' Christ, in our sanctuary, is found the fullness of the light and glory of the Godhead.

In the image, it's as though everything upon the altar is engulfed in a flame which burns so brightly that it reaches even beyond the roof of the church. This is the 'fire' of Christ's praise of the Father; and it reaches as far as Heaven.

We who are privileged to kneel and pray before Christ should rejoice in our Faith. Christ can help us to be faithful to the end; and so we should come to Him as often as we can, to benefit from His Real Presence, which makes the sanctuary resemble a blazing furnace: an area in which the fire of love is burning fiercely and is pouring out graces from the Godhead. We need only place ourselves before this 'fire' (Heb 12:29), in order to benefit. We need never worry about whether our prayers are 'worthy' of our Saviour. Every sincere prayer delights Him; so we can rest quietly before Him, in silent homage. In this way, we can allow Him to 'irradiate' us with His glory, which is the glory, also, of the Father and of the Holy Spirit.

This 'fire' of Christ's praise pours out ceaselessly from every tabernacle in the world where Christ is sacramentally Present; and we who treasure Christ's Real Presence amongst us have a wonderful opportunity by which to remind ourselves of Christ's love for us, to rededicate ourselves to His service, and to unite our hearts' praises, in the Spirit, with Christ's praise of the Father's infinite glory.

(Text adapted from *Teachings in Prayer Volume Four*, T:2138 of 16.2.97)

If we kneel before Christ, Who is sacramentally Present,
it's as if we allow Him to irradiate us with His glory.
(OIL-S:2138)

93

OUR 'HOMELAND'.

At every second of our earthly life, we are on a journey: a spiritual journey. Though always held 'in' God and sustained by Him, we are in some manner either moving closer towards Him or turning away from His face. How important it is, therefore, to do all we can to remain in His love, and to show love towards our neighbour.

God the Father delights in our longing to know Him, and draws us further into His life the more generously we co-operate with His graces. The Father delights in our faith, and in our gratitude to Him for His gifts: for life and faith and every blessing - and for Christ, His Son, Whom He sent down to earth to die for us.

The little figure in the picture is being powerfully drawn into God's heart, by God's power, swept towards Him as if towards the heart of a whirlpool, or as if in a whirlwind of love, or a storm of rejoicing. True friends of God who are living in God are as if soaring within His being, in everyday life and in prayer. They are at peace in His love, and are united with Him in every act, thought and intention.

God the Holy Trinity is the 'heart' from which we were born. In Him, we dwell in friendship. He is the 'homeland' (Ph 3:20) in which we can move in freedom. He is the infinite torrent of light and joy in which we can soar, in prayer. He is the goal of our yearning hearts. He is the destination at which, through our life 'in Christ' and our union, we already arrive. He is the love in which we are held, safely. He is the Breath which we breathe, in His embrace. He is the 'playground' for us, His children, as - in silent prayer - we search, enraptured, in the vast, soaring heights of His infinite love, in safety.

(Adapted from *Teachings in Prayer Volume Four,* T:2169 of 23.3.97)

Whoever is united to God in every act, thought and
intention, is drawn to Him in a whirlwind of love.
(OIL-S:2169)

MUTUAL GIVING AND RECEIVING.

The life of the Holy Trinity is ours to share, through our Baptism, and even ours to enjoy in a known and blissful manner. If we persevere in love, and nourish our 'life in Christ' through the sacraments, prove our love for Christ by loving our neighbour, and grow close to Christ in prayer, we can be drawn by Christ, even in this life - in prayer - into the heart of the Godhead. Then at last we realise, clearly, that the Three Who are so powerful and majestic are at the same time gentle, sweet, consoling, palpably 'present' to the soul, and infinitely kind and patient.

As we begin to grow used to our undeserved yet blissful interior life, we find that Christ delights in our gratitude for everything good, and wants us to continue to put our trust in Him and in His plans.

Through Him we have been drawn into the real intimacy with the Holy Trinity: one God, yet Three Persons, to Whom we offer our life, in willing service; and when the 'nights' of darkness have ended, we find the joy and glory and fulfilment for which we have been yearning. We learn that that joy and glory are the 'climate' which is enjoyed by everyone who lives 'in' God, in true union.

We can say that God is wholly 'occupied' with love. The three Divine Persons - The Holy Trinity - are 'occupied' in a ceaseless, unbroken, and blissful mutual giving and receiving of perfect love, 'in' joy and glory; and whoever consents to God's love and action is drawn into the heart of the Godhead. It is as though, in prayer, we are leaping, joyfully - even now, in earthly life - into the bliss and glory of the Divine life of the Holy Trinity: the one eternal God Who can be our eternal delight and joy.

(Adapted from *Teachings in Prayer Volume Four,* T:2221 of 25.5.97)

Through our prayers, we can leap joyfully
into the life of the Holy Trinity.
(OIL-S:2221)

AS IF WITHIN A DEEP OCEAN.

Everyone who lives 'in' God, and immerses himself in God in prayer, is as if bathing in a deep ocean of charity.

The little figure in the picture has leapt into prayer, in trust; and his faith tells him that whether he experiences peace in prayer, or is battered by distractions or temptations, he is nevertheless supported and loved by the Holy Trinity: by the Father, the Son and the Holy Spirit. They are at work in his life and in his soul.

None of us can imagine how deep are the depths of God's love for us; yet He wants us to grow in faith so that we'll believe in His love in every circumstance and every difficulty; and He wants us to grow in knowledge about Him, so that we'll be full of wonder at what He does for us. That's why we should always remember that God is One but Three, and that we who have been brought to live at the heart of Divine life now live at the heart of the Most Holy Trinity.

We know that Christ is the 'way' to eternal life in God (Jn 14:6); and we know that when we meet Christ in Holy Communion we also meet the Father and the Holy Spirit, Who are distinct from one another and from Christ, yet Who are always united with one another and with Him; and so we enjoy an intimate and loving Communion with the Three Divine Persons; and whoever knows this is and is grateful can be sure that every time he offers a new expression of praise, reverence or gratitude to God, he is being drawn even further into the depths of God's infinite grace and goodness.

(Adapted from *Teachings in Prayer Volume Four,* T:2343 of 5.10.97)

Whoever immerses himself in God, in prayer,
is as if bathing in a deep ocean of charity.
(OIL-S:2343)

99

SPIRITUAL 'SHELTER' IN THE CHURCH.

The infinite goodness of God is beyond our imagination. His immense charity and holiness are so great that we cannot understand them. We cannot picture His purity, or His infinite beauty. We cannot comprehend His Being. It's as though He is light - although invisible; or it's as though He is 'fire' (Dt 4:24) - yet invisible; and He is infinite, unchanging, never-ending love.

Furthermore, it's as if, in His power and majesty, God now fills with His presence the entire church building in which we worship; and at the same time - as in the picture - it's as though the building is completely enveloped and 'held' in God and in the pure fire of His holiness just as a little scrap of paper is enveloped and 'held' as it floats upon the billowing flames of a blazing bonfire. 'For our God is a consuming fire' (Heb 12:29).

We can see, through this illustration, how God protects us all, because of His love for us. The little church building symbolises the power and purpose of the living Church - the Mystical Body of Christ - into which God has called us. We who worship together 'in' Christ and with Him, today, can believe that we are 'sheltered', so to speak, during earthly life, by the gifts which Christ gives us through His Church. It's as though we can find spiritual shelter in the peace and security of the sacraments of the Church, until the time when - if we are sufficiently purified - we can enter unafraid, after death, into the fire of God's infinite love: into the glory of the most Holy Trinity.

(Adapted from *Teachings in Prayer Volume Five*, T:2521 of 27.2.98)

The Church's sacraments give us peace and security,
as we enter the light and fire of Divine love.
(OIL-S:2521)

BY THE SPIRIT'S POWER.

If we have entered the life of the Godhead, and long to stay in that light and bliss forever, and yet are tempted to lose hope, as we consider our sins and weaknesses, we must never forget that God Himself - God the Son, made flesh - has entered our world and shared our life, to help and to save us.

In His human nature, Christ has suffered as we do, though He was sinless; yet we understand Him better if we remember that, although He emptied Himself of glory, for our sakes, He was never separated from the Father and the Holy Spirit.

Christ is true God and true man; and even when He prayed in torment in Gethsemane, during His life on earth, aware of the horrors that lay ahead, He was held in the Father's love. He was supported by the Holy Spirit, Who enabled Him to rise up and move forward to endure mockery and shame, and to take up His Cross, and so fulfil the Father's Will for Him.

By His self-sacrifice, Christ bridged the Abyss between Mankind and the Godhead. He made a way back to Heaven, so that all who acknowledge Him as their Saviour can share His life, be reconciled to the Father, and hope to enter Heaven, at life's end; and the Holy Spirit Who fortified Him can powerfully fortify us. He can enable us to rise up and fulfil the Father's Will, each time we face a new difficulty: provided we don't try to rely on our own strength, but trust in His power and His love.

(Text adapted from *Teachings in Prayer Volume Five*, T:2528 of 3.3.98)

*We can be strengthened and consoled by the very Spirit
Who upheld Christ in Gethsemane and on the Cross.*
(OIL-S:2528)

THE FATHER'S LOVE.

Who can describe the Father's love for us? In Christ we see that love shown out to us, as we see Christ speaking and healing, raising to life, consoling, and bringing peace and forgiveness; and in the Sacred Scriptures we hear God's love for us described as being like the love which a Bridegroom has for His bride, or a King for His subjects - or a mother for the infant on her lap (Is 49:15); and if we sometimes find it hard to believe in that love, when we look at our own sinfulness, or at the terrors and tragedies in human societies, we can remind ourselves of what we've learned from Holy Scripture - and from the Sacred Tradition of the Church, through the words and witness of many of our Christian forebears who have spoken with joy about life 'in Christ' (2 Co 5:17).

We are told that all who allow themselves to be led by the Spirit through trials and persecutions, and through the 'desolate wastes' of interior darkness, in purification, will find rest in God, eventually, in the pure silence and bliss of contemplation. Those who have experienced the felt-love of God can say that the Holy Spirit stops our words, it seems, as He bestows His gift to the soul of pure, interior joy, with extraordinary peace, and the knowledge of being loved.

It's as though the Father, by the Spirit's touch, is reaching out to the soul: to a person who has been changed and transformed, through Christ, to become a true child of God; and, in this sort of prayer - as shown in the illustration - it's as if the Father holds his 'baby' on his lap. The Father's love for the soul is so great that He delights in her life, and in her closeness to Him; and so He fondles her head, and runs His fingers through her little curls: such is the sort of intimacy with our God which is achieved in the heights of contemplation.

In earlier encounters with God the soul was overwhelmed by the contrast between God's holiness and her sinfulness; yet now her fear has turned to joy.

(Adapted from *Teachings in Prayer Volume Five*, T:2550 of 18.3.98)

The Father's tender, consoling love is experienced by
privileged souls in the heights of contemplation.
(OIL-S:2550)

'SHIELDED' BY CHRIST.

As we grow in the knowledge and love of God, we learn to keep our 'balance', so to speak: to trust in His infinitely tender and personal love for us, whilst approaching Him with reverence and awe. We open our hearts to God with confidence, whilst remaining aware that no lips can speak praise which is worthy of God the Father unless that praise is offered through Jesus Christ His Son, in the Spirit.

The painting illustrates the fact that, for worthy prayer, we all need Christ, the God-man: our Redeemer and High Priest. If mere words are addressed to the Godhead by a frail creature, with merely human power, those words are like dry leaves which are swept away, as if in an almighty gale, by the powerful currents in the furnace of Divine glory. Christ alone, by His purity and power, can hold each willing soul in the overwhelming radiance and purity and power of the life of the Godhead. No-one but He, Who is God: pure, holy and powerful, is 'strong' enough to stand before the Father, to bring us close to Him and yet to 'shield' us, as we are praying, from the 'fire' of the Father's love.

In order to bear the sight of the Father's glory, or of the radiance of His Son, we must be made like Christ through prayer, and through His gift of Himself to us in Holy Communion. Then we can gaze upon the Divine radiance within our souls: upon the light of the Holy Spirit Who dwells within the soul of each true friend of Christ. That radiance shines out towards the Father as from a mirror, when - after necessary purifications - we mirror Christ's beauty and reflect that beauty towards the Father. In this way, the Father receives from us frail creatures, as our own gifts to Him, infinitely-glorious homage and praise. In giving Christ's glory to the Father in such a holy and spiritual way we offer praise which is worthy of Heaven. We have praise which is 'powerful' enough to ascend within the furnace of love in the glory of the Godhead; and it is praise which cannot be swept aside, but which always reaches the Father's 'heart' (Jn 1:18).

(Adapted from *Teachings in Prayer Volume Five*, T:2551 of 18.3.98)

No-one but Christ, our Divine Saviour, can bring
us close to the burning 'fire' of the Father's love.
(OIL-S:2551)

ACROSS THE ABYSS.

In advancing from one stage to another throughout our 'life in Christ' we become more and more aware of our lack of virtue, our poor understanding of the things of God, our ingratitude for the many gifts we take for granted - and our need of purification; yet the mature soul is growing in wisdom; and she knows - with all these new insights into truth - the truth about God's ceaseless and perfect love for her.

At last, she believes with all her heart that it is the eternal desire of God, Who is infinitely generous and good, to make Himself known to each one of us and therefore both to give and to receive love. She learns, by experience, that whoever responds to His love, and endures all sorts of trials and episodes of spiritual darkness, eventually leads a life of perpetual inner joy, and is lost in wonder at His invisible majesty and glory. She marvels at the knowledge that God chooses to share His life with 'mere' creatures. She learns that, all the time, God delights in sharing His knowledge of Himself with her soul.

Now she can speak with confidence to other people, telling them that God lavishes gifts upon every creature, because He is good; yet He lavishes His extraordinary gifts upon those who have trusted in Christ, His Son, and who have relied upon the power and love of the Holy Spirit in order to become more 'conformed' to Christ in obedience and love; and amongst the extraordinary 'sights' which can be given in the heights of the spiritual life are glimpses not of God's face, but of His eternal radiant light. The fortunate soul can say, from experience, that such depths of knowledge are achieved in and through Christ; and whoever is enabled, thus, by a spiritual gift or faculty, to gaze - so to speak - across the Abyss which separates Mankind from the Godhead, enjoys a brief glimpse of the radiance which veils the Father, the Son and the Holy Spirit: thus enjoying not a glimpse of the One, Holy God, Whom we cannot yet see, but a glimpse of His undying and everlasting Triune glory.

(Adapted from *Teachings in Prayer Volume Five*, T:2670 of 6.6.98)

Through contemplative prayer, a soul might gain,
across the Abyss, a glimpse of the Triune glory.
(OIL-S:2670)

THE HOLY TRINITY AT WORK.

The Three Divine Persons are Three-in-One: one and active. The Father sustains us all in existence. Christ reaches down to save us. The Holy Spirit guides and sanctifies our souls; so this image is like a diagram of the Holy Trinity at work. This sphere represents the unity and holiness of the Godhead, and God's eternal work of love.

The Father's life is indicated by the head at the top of the picture. At the centre of the sphere is an opening which represents the Father's 'heart' (Jn 1:18), and a figure can be seen leaping out from the centre. This represents the eternal 'procession' of the Son, the Word, Who is eternally engendered, we say, from the Father. Christ is seen leaping out as if from the Father's heart - as we say in the Creed: "God from God, and light from light" (CCC:197). Christ leaves His glory behind Him, propelled by love, to become man; and He dives outwards so powerfully that He breaks free from the sphere to plunge down towards people who live in darkness: to die for us sinners, to save us from eternal death.

The right of the sphere is half-encircled by the upward flight of a third figure, which represents the Holy Spirit. He shares the wondrous interior life of the Godhead; yet He too is 'at work', as He sanctifies and draws Heavenwards those whom the Father has called and to whom Christ His Son has reached out through His Incarnation. It is the Father's plan that Christ will gather together in love all who are willing to put their trust in Him. Father, Son and Holy Spirit work as one, to draw frail creatures into Their blissful embrace, and to share Their Divine life forever. Truly, the Father is the Origin of all life, light and love; and His loving Son could not have failed to come out from the Father's heart, to save us; and the Holy Spirit is the Person and the power by Whom sinful persons can be transformed and lifted up to Heaven; yet the Three Divine Persons are one, and work as one: always active in the great, holy work of love in Eternity, in the eternal 'dance' and delight of Heaven.

(Text adapted from *Teachings in Prayer Volume Five*, T:2731 of 23.7.98)

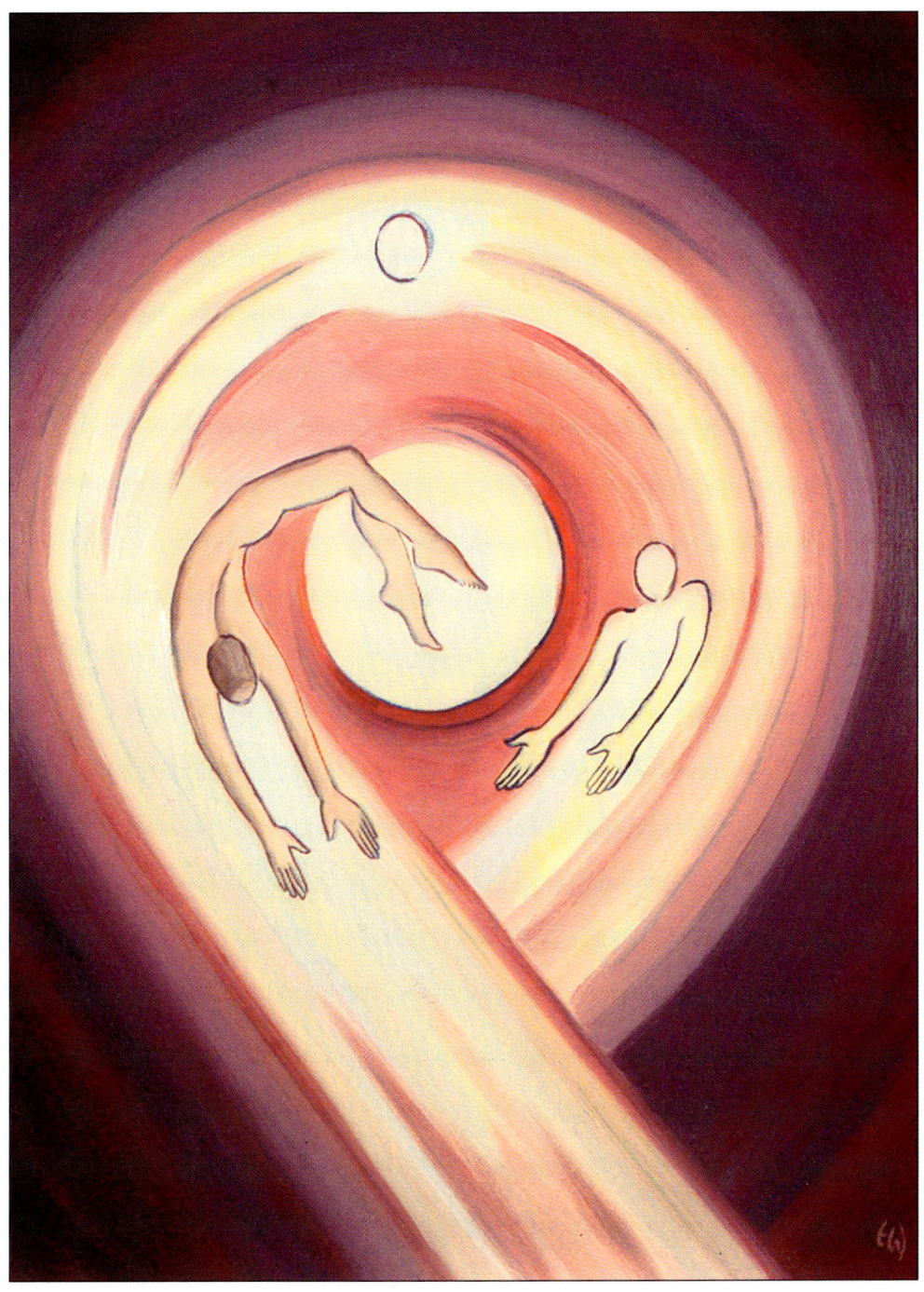

Christ left behind His glory, to plunge down to earth,
to save us who live in darkness.
(OIL-S:2731)

111

THE SAVING EVENTS.

The Three Divine Persons are 'at work' to save and sanctify us through the sacraments, today; and They do so supremely through the Holy Sacrifice of the Mass, at which Christ's saving sacrifice of Calvary is re-presented and at which we receive Christ Himself as our spiritual Food. We are doing something powerfully fruitful and effective whenever come together in this way, as the 'Body of Christ'. We know, by faith, in a way beyond human understanding, that the Father to Whom we pray through Christ, at the Mass, contains and sustains all things; and our understanding of this can be increased through prayer. If He 'contains' everything that is, He 'contains' the risen Christ, 'in' Whom can now be found Christ's Passion, Death, Resurrection and Ascension: the work of our salvation.

This paschal work is illustrated opposite, where Christ wears on His breast an image of His Cross and His tomb, and of the places where He preached in Galilee. It's as if everyone who is incorporated into Christ can therefore touch and be changed by the saving events of Christ's life, and so can hope to achieve salvation.

We know that to belong to Christ, Who lives at the Father's 'heart,' is to be changed by His work and also to be 'held' by Him close to the Father; so whoever ignores Christ cannot be close to the Father. It's true that everyone on earth is in the Father's care in earthly life; yet whoever refuses to meet or to know Christ, Mankind's Saviour, and so refuses to allow Christ to change, sanctify and save him, is in danger. When he dies he is not - by his own choice - 'held' in Christ as if in the Father's heart; and so he falls away into the Abyss. That's why the Church continually reminds us that only in Christ have we the sure hope of remaining 'in' the Father, after our death, and in His tender love, saved by Christ by the Redeemer in Whom we have put our trust. To achieve salvation, it is necessary that we have faith, and that our faith be alive and active.

(Text adapted from *Teachings in Prayer Volume Six (unpublished,)* T:2772 of 25.8.98)

In the Risen Christ Who lives at the Father's
heart we can find Christ's entire paschal work.
(OIL-S:2772)

113

CHRIST AT THE CENTRE.

When we have realised our need of Christ, and our need of His gifts and graces, we receive Him as frequently as possible in the Holy Eucharist, and in other sacraments. We know that Christ delights in coming to His friends in Holy Communion; and He delights in our praise - as does the Holy Spirit, and our Father in Heaven.

The triple light which is pictured here is a symbol of the Godhead. Christ stands at the centre, radiant with glory. He is true man: risen and glorified; yet He is also true God, and therefore equal in majesty to the almighty, invisible Father, and to the Holy Spirit. That's why we celebrate with gladness, each year, the feast of the Holy Trinity, even if we don't yet understand the depths of this holy Mystery. This is a day of especial joy for Christ, who shares His own glory with His friends by setting each of those souls on fire during the Mass or during Exposition of the Blessed Sacrament, making souls radiant with His Divine and holy light.

We need never be ashamed to admit that we need Christ our Saviour. He loves us; and He can help us to be faithful to the end; and so we should frequently approach Him, to benefit from His Real Presence. We need never worry about the 'quality' of our prayers - as long as they are sincere, and as long as our central desire is for truth and goodness. Christ is deeply touched by our trust, if we approach Him with open hearts, to share our thoughts with Him, or simply to rest in His Presence.

We mustn't imagine that we have to use words in an attempt to bind ourselves closer to Christ. He is Really Present with us in a wonderful manner, both in our Holy Communion, and when the Blessed Sacrament is exposed in the monstrance on the altar. He sees our hearts' true intentions; and we can rest quietly before Him, or turn our heart towards Him, in a moment of silent homage.

(Adapted from *Volume Seven of Teachings in Prayer (unpublished)*, T:3067 of 30.5.99, and from *of Teachings in Prayer Volume Four*, T:2143 of 23.2.97)

Christ lives in Heaven, in radiant glory; and He is equal
in majesty to the Father and the Holy Spirit.
(OIL-S:3067)

'FROM HIS SANCTUARY'.

Every blessing which we now receive through Christ's Church has come to us because Christ was made incarnate of the Virgin Mary, in order to die for our sins. It was as though the Father had 'leaned down' from his sanctuary on high 'That he might hear the groans of the prisoners and free those condemned to die' (Ps 102:18-20);   and so He sent His own Son to live amongst sinful people, in a darkened world, to free us from sin and from the fear of death.

In the image, it's as though the Father, Whose heart is so loving, was deeply touched to see a man - albeit His own Son - in whom there was no shadow of selfishness,   nor any self-pity, nor any rebellion against the Father even during heartache and suffering; and yet the wonderful sight which the Father once saw as He gazed at the pure loving heart of Christ during Christ's life on Earth - even during Christ's Passion - is still seen by the Father today, as He gazes upon earth; and this is because Christ remains amongst His People today through His sacramental Presence; and therefore Christ praises and thanks the Father today, from upon Earth, as He once praised and thanked Him during His earthly life - even from the Cross.

As brothers and sisters of Christ, we pray immensely noble and powerful prayers. If we are united with Christ as He praises the Father today, on earth - during the Mass - we make Christ's praise our own. The Father hears our words with as much delight as He hears Christ's words; and this is because we speak and pray 'in Christ'; and so it is with sufferings as well as prayers, when we do penance to help other people. Such is the wonderful way of life to which we are called, through having been made 'children of God'.

(Text adapted from a further unpublished Teaching, T:3105 of 23.6.99)

The Father saw Christ's pure love shining out from the Cross; and
He sees that light today wherever Christ is sacramentally Present.
(OIL-S:3105)

ETERNALLY PROCEEDING.

It is a wondrous mystery, that the Second Person of the Holy Trinity - the Son of God - is both God and man. True God, He now shares our human nature - all because He once came 'out' from the Father's heart. He is all 'light', in His perfect holiness, yet He was made flesh by the Spirit's power, so that He could share our life on earth. He bore the torments inflicted upon Him by sinful people. He was sinless, and yet He prayed for sinners, so that everyone who is willing to 'run' to Him and share His life can live in His light and have all sins forgiven, and even rise up, in the end, to share His glory in Heaven.

Yet when we reflect on what Christ has done for us by leaving behind His glory - leaving it for a short time, long ago - we realise that His life in the Godhead is not now 'static'. Though His descent to earth and His triumphant return to the Father have been accomplished, Christ has not ceased to act in love. We can say that He proceeds eternally from the Father, within the Godhead. He is "eternally begotten of the Father", as we say in the Creed: "God from God, Light from Light."

Christ is perpetually the Father's Word, offered until the end of time as a generous gift to all who will receive His Spirit in Baptism and Confirmation, and His Body and Blood in the sacrament of the Holy Eucharist; yet Christ is perpetually one with the Father and the Holy Spirit. He never 'leaves' them. There is, in the Godhead, no beginning and no end, but only a perpetual, mutual-expression of love. It is true that the Three Divine Persons are equal in majesty and holiness and love, yet we can say that the Father is the Source from Whom proceeds the Son; and with Them, in one unending embrace, is the Holy Spirit. The procession of Persons in the Holy Trinity is eternally 'proceeding,' since the unity and oneness and love and work of the Godhead are eternal.

(Text adapted from an unpublished Teaching, T:3198 of 26.6.99)

*The Son is ''eternally begotten'' of the Father: eternally
proceeding, in the oneness and love of the Godhead.*
(OIL-S:3198)

ALL CREATION: 'IN' GOD.

There is a danger, as we think about God, of imagining that the created world is God. The beauties of the earth powerfully reflect His beauty. The laws of physics reflect His wisdom; and when we consider the development of life in a hundred thousand forms we are filled with awe at God's magnificence and generosity. Yet the created Universe remains His Creation. It is not Divine, but was created from nothing. All its beauty is borrowed, so to speak, though we know that when God made the Universe, 'God saw that it was good' (Gn 1:21). Nothing in Creation lies 'outside' His love.

We can say that God is 'in' Creation in the sense that He is omnipresent; and yet we can know that the whole of Creation is 'in' Him - as illustrated opposite in a literalistic way, where the earth and the depth of space are seen as if 'contained' in Christ's heart.

We can say with confidence that everything that is good has sprung from God's heart. He is our Lord and Creator; and it is the Will of God that we know about His Triune life and work, and know that He holds us all in existence. He invites us all to share in His blissful life.

Whoever freely chooses to become a true friend of God lives at God's 'heart', so to speak, even during earthly life, through Christ's merits and the Spirit's love. We can be sure, furthermore, that God holds and cherishes now in a special way, in His heart, all who have died and gone to Him because they had not utterly and eternally rejected Him. Those wise and happy souls have freely decided to follow the way of faith and love and self-giving.

(Adapted from an unpublished Teaching, T:3247 of 6.10.99)

God is 'in' Creation, by His omnipresence; yet
all that He has made is 'held' in His care.
(OIL-S:3247)

A GRADUAL REVELATION.

There is no love to match the Father's love: no tenderness or sweetness on Earth as tender and sweet as His love towards us; yet we can say that His pure love is like a raging fire: like the 'refiner's fire' of Holy Scripture (Ml 3:2). It is so radiantly pure and powerful that whoever meets Him unprepared would be frightened and harmed by such contact. Only after our purification and transformation do we 'taste' and enjoy Divine sweetness.

If we bear in mind God's immense glory and the frailty of sinful human beings, we can see that God revealed Himself to His Chosen People in the only possible way. He revealed Himself little by little, through gentle words and invitations, then also through signs and wonders and warnings. Thus, He taught us all about the astonishing juxtaposition, in Himself, of tenderness and Majesty.

We can picture some of those people of ancient times as they stand in a desert and gaze into the distance. They have learned that God is like a mighty fire of love, which blazes for mile upon mile. It's as if God keeps Himself almost hidden from man's sight, beyond a range of mountains, since to approach human beings just as He is, in His Divine glory, would destroy them; yet God is preparing them for a later time. At last, God wonderfully chose to come amongst us, to teach us about Himself. He did so 'when the appointed time came' (Ga 4:4), at a particular place, through Christ His Son, Who is true God: the Son of the Father. Christ is God-made-man. He is love incarnate: love embodied and so made visible.

Whoever is full of wonder that the fire of love came amongst us on earth will marvel more on realising that the people who met Jesus were 'shielded' by His humanity from His Divine glory - except, for example, at His Transfiguration, when that glory awed the Apostles. What can any true believer do, except honour and serve Him Who was raised from the dead, and Who awaits us in Heaven?

(Adapted from an unpublished Teaching, T:3319 of 11.11.99)

God's love is sweet and tender, yet also fiery and powerful;
so He has revealed Himself little by little.
(OIL-S:3319)

123

A REFLECTION OF DIVINE LOVE. (1)

Just as God, because of His generous and loving nature, cannot fail to share His love and light and glory, so those who genuinely hope to resemble Him are always burning to share their joy: to speak about God's love for us and about the forgiveness of our sins.

The mutual self-bestowal of the Three Divine Persons is mirrored in human life where souls work together for God's glory. As Divine life comes to fruition in a soul who loves God profoundly, that soul cannot contain his delight. He must share his joy, and speak to other people about the delight and fulfilment which he has found in God. He must share the joy which has come to him in contemplation; and therefore he works fervently to draw other souls towards true fulfilment: towards true union with God.

If we consider the work of the Holy Trinity, and see that work expressed in diagrammatic form (- with the Father at the apex of a triangle, and the Son and the Holy Spirit at lower left and right respectively -) we can say that the Father's love is perpetually poured out on the Son, Who is 'the image of the unseen God' (Col 1:15-29); and thus the Father is revealed, through the Son, to those whom He has chosen. The Son perpetually adores the Father, and intercedes with Him for His 'children' (Ro 8:16); and the Father, with the Son, pours out the Spirit upon the chosen; and the Spirit causes them to love the Son and to praise the Father's goodness. Furthermore, Spirit and Son are united in love, and are one with the Father; and thus the 'circle' of love is complete, yet not closed. True charity is not exclusive, but must share joy; and that is why chosen souls are all the while being prompted and inspired by God, and are being drawn up high into the light of God. A similar pattern can be seen as certain privileged souls are drawn into God's work: and this can be seen overleaf in diagram 2, where the form of the triangle is used again, to explain God's work in faithful souls.

(Adapted from an unpublished Teaching T:3466 of 19.1.00)

The Three Divine Persons are one in love; yet
They are reaching out in love, to us 'below.'
(OIL-S:3466A)

A REFLECTION OF DIVINE LOVE. (2)

In this second diagram, we can place the Holy Spirit - Whom we can describe as the agent of change for the Holy Trinity - at the Apex. At the lower left and right, respectively, we can place two of Christ's true friends: A and B, who, in their relationship with the Godhead, mirror the work of the Three Divine Persons - as it's just been described, in diagram 1.

We can consider the process of conversion and sharing as being a 'reflection' of the life of the Holy Trinity. Let us describe such a process by saying that the Holy Spirit is perpetually pouring out His love upon A, who responds to that love, is converted and transformed, and longs to reveal the Spirit's love and beauty to other people. This friend of God, A, perpetually adores the Holy Spirit - and the Father and the Son - and intercedes on behalf of other souls; and the Holy Spirit, acting with and for A, pours out Divine life upon another person, B, thus causing him to be grateful to A for having drawn down God's grace upon him and also causing him to praise the Holy Spirit for His goodness. Furthermore - still mirroring the first image - A and B are firmly united in a spiritual bond. They are as one, in their aim to love and to do the Will of the Spirit. They know that He is the Source of their wisdom and joy; so each inspires the other towards greater love for God and to greater heights of virtue; and thus, this circle of love too is completed, yet not closed, since other souls - chosen by Providence - are all the while being called and inspired both by A and by B, to emerge from darkness and to enter God's light. Then they, too, on sharing God's life and being transformed, will reach out to other people; so the work of A can be seen as a pattern for priestly ministry, in that it reproduces Christ's priestly ministry. By his priestly work, A helps B towards God and towards true freedom and fulfilment; thus, B is helped to help others; and God is glorified by the loving, selfless work of A, the praise and gratitude of B, and the work of both, as they reach out to inspire other people to praise God and to spread the Gospel.

(Adapted from an unpublished Teaching, T:3466 of 19.1.00)

In drawing one another towards God, Christ's
friends mirror the work of the Holy Trinity.
(OIL-S:3466B)

THE COMMUNION OF SAINTS.

Everyone on earth who is truly 'in communion' with Christ and His Church through being 'alight' with the Holy Spirit, given in Baptism, is therefore 'in communion' with the Saints of Heaven who live in God's light, and with the Holy Souls who are being purified; and this is true even if he cannot yet see them. He knows this through faith.

As faintly indicated in the painting, the glory of the Saints of Heaven is so great that it's as though, in their Heavenly beauty and transformation, they form a corona or brilliant setting for the dazzling 'jewel' of the Godhead; yet they are 'in communion' with weak, sinful people like ourselves. They live with Christ in glory, yet they are very close to us. They pray for us. They love to hear our prayers and fulfil our confident requests. Most of all, they love to see us grow in charity: to see us love Christ, and, for His sake, show love for our neighbour.

Through the sure bond of charity and spiritual communion we have a means of finding reliable and frequent help amongst earthly troubles. If we ask the Saints for help, and celebrate the Saints' feast days, and even yearn to be with them in glory, we are nurturing real friendships between the Saints and ourselves; and these friendships will be marvellously fulfilled when we reach Heaven. We too can hope to please God and give Him glory forever, just as they do; and when we arrive in Heaven, we'll enjoy meeting, at last, all these wonderful friends who have been briefly 'veiled' from our sight.

The Most Holy Trinity in Whom the Saints now live is one God, invisible, majestic, wise and omnipotent: the Source of all Heavenly beauty, the Giver of Heavenly glory, the Cause of the bliss which the Saints enjoy in Heaven, and the Source of the joy which is given to those who persevere through all difficulties, on the narrow way opened up by Christ.

(Adapted from an unpublished Teaching, T:3768 of 9.5.00)

*Even now, Christ's friends are one in the Communion
of Saints, who form a 'corona' round the Godhead.*
(OIL-S:3768)

LIKE A TRIPLE 'WHEEL' OF FIRE.

Every true friend of Christ longs to urge other people towards holiness and true joy - perhaps by speaking or writing about the bliss and glory of Heaven; yet whoever speaks or writes about union with God must say that preparation is essential for all who hope to enter the blissful 'fire' which is Divine love.

The fiery purity of the Godhead can be pictured as being like the burning radiance of a huge, triple wheel of fire, rather like a huge nebula at the edge of which stands a small figure. Here is someone prayerful whose soul has been thoroughly purified by the work of the Holy Spirit.

Every loving soul who hopes to meet God in an intimate and tender union must undergo a thorough preparation, or the undimmed vision of the glory and majesty of the Triune God would be unbearable.

Each soul must be made 'like' God - deified or divinised, as we say - through being spiritually transformed and made like God, in love; and this is achieved during earthly life, through the sacraments and through penances, purification and spiritual transformation, or after death, through the purifications of Purgatory.

What an extraordinary way of life is achieved, however, by those few who, even in this life, have completed their purifications, and who therefore enjoy many of the gifts enjoyed by those who have reached Heaven. Even here on earth, they rest in the heart of the Holy Trinity in prayer, share and experience Divine peace, joy, sweetness, light and glory, converse with the Saints, their true friends, look in wonder at the holy Angels who guard them, and offer fervent thanks to God each day for having delivered them from their earlier way of life, and also for having delivered them from the fear of death.

(Adapted from an unpublished Teaching, T:3884 of 27.6.00)

Purification and deification are necessary for all
who want to enter the pure fire of the Godhead.
(OIL-S:3884)

REACHING OUT IN LOVE.

It's a marvellous moment, when we realise the meaning and purpose of Christ's Passion, Death, Resurrection and Ascension: His whole paschal work. The entire plan of salvation effected by God - by Father, Son and Holy Spirit - has sprung from God's love for us. Truly, Christ the Son died to save us; and so we pray in Christ's name to the Father during the Mass, to say, of Christ's sacrifice, "Father ... accept this offering from your whole family. Grant us peace in this life. Save us from final damnation; and count us among those you have chosen;" and we can be confident that the Son of God, Who poured out His blood on Calvary, to save us, will give us every help and encouragement to remain faithful to Him until death.

In the image on page 135 it's as if the Divine Son in Heaven has just spoken to His Father about all that He, the Son, will suffer when He 'descends' to become man, in a cruel world. The Son is full of love for sinful people on earth who are alienated from the Father because of their sins. They have no hope of Heaven, even though some of them are contrite and make good but inadequate gestures of love for God, and submit to His Holy Will, for example, by fasting, prayer and alms-giving, and by offering animal sacrifices; yet these things alone cannot take away their sins. It's as though the Son asks His Father's permission to go down to earth in order to help and save sinners. There, the Son, enfleshed, will live amongst them. He will live as they live, yet without sinning; and He will accept the sufferings which are inevitable if He lives a life of love and truth-speaking in a sinful world: a life of faithfulness to the Father's Will in every circumstance.

The Son will even accept death - a cruel death - if it should occur. By that patient acceptance He will demonstrate to Mankind how love conquers fear: true love for God the Father and for His Will, which is that all people live in love together as children of one Father. Yet something even more marvellous will ensue. The Son knows that the Father won't allow Him - His only Son - to remain in the grave, but will lift Him up again by the power of the Holy Spirit; and in the Son's laying-down of His life, and the Father's raising-up of the Son from the grave, They will demonstrate that darkness cannot conquer light.

Furthermore, as the Son pours out His blood in death, He will be shedding it out of love for Mankind, since, if He didn't love, He would hate and revile and kill those who oppose Him. He would shed their blood rather than be humiliated and defeated; yet as the Son pours out His blood on the Cross, He will be shedding it for love of His Father since if He didn't love His Father and His Father's eternal 'law' of love He wouldn't endure suffering in order to speak the truth, to do good, and to do His duty to the bitter end. Therefore, as the Son sheds His blood, out of love for God and man, in total self-giving, He will know that His freely-accepted death can be seen as the last and most perfect blood-sacrifice for sin. In pouring out His blood - as is inevitable, in a sinful world - He will make a new covenant: a new agreement between Mankind and God the Father.

Since the Son will be amongst sinners and will numbered amongst them through having been made man - though without sin - in Mary's womb, He will pray heart-felt prayers for their salvation; and He will do so even when they are crucifying Him; and since the Father always grants the prayers of His Son, it is plain that the Son, as He sheds His blood on the Cross, will seal by that blood a new covenant between the human beings for whom He prays - whom He will represent as their spokesman - and the Father in Heaven; and a covenant which has been sealed in the blood of the only Son of God, and not in the blood of an animal, will be a covenant so powerful that nothing shall ever break it.

So now it is plain that God's whole plan of salvation has stemmed from love. No blood-sacrifice was necessary to placate an angry tyrant. God is wholly love and light. A blood sacrifice was freely offered, by the loving, incarnate Son, Jesus, in His own body, with the 'consent' or Will of the Father, in the love of the Holy Spirit.

We read in Holy Scripture each year, on the feast of the Annunciation, what St. Paul wrote, of Christ: "this is what Christ said, on coming into the world: You who wanted no sacrifice or oblation prepared a body for me ... God, here I am! I am coming to obey your will' (Heb 10:4-7); then St Paul continues: '... this will was for us to be made holy by the offering of his body made once and for all by Jesus Christ' (Heb 10:10).

In the illustration opposite, Christ already knows that when He has died, and has risen from the dead, and has ascended to Heaven, many people will learn from His disciples about what He has done for them by His loving sacrifice. People who are grateful and who recognise their sinfulness will want to change: willing to die to themselves, as the Son has done. All who are willing to repent and to believe, and therefore to receive the Holy Spirit as they undergo the mystical death and rising in the waters of Baptism, will thus be reconciled with the Father. They can share the Son's Divine life through eating the spiritual Food which is His Eucharistic Body and Blood, and therefore hope to come to Heaven, one day, through the Son, in the Spirit, to live in bliss forever, close to the Father's heart. Now it is plain why - in the image - the Father is seen reaching out with infinite love and tenderness to touch and embrace the Son Who kneels before Him. With that touch, the Father expresses His consent to the proposed course of action. He gives His blessing upon the whole plan. As the Father leans towards His Son in love, that 'reaching-out' in infinite love is the Holy Spirit. That love is so pure and powerful and holy that It - He - is One of Three Divine Persons Who eternally love and are loved - One God - in Heaven. The Holy Spirit is like a burning fire in His purity and fervour: always longing to give joy. He is a love so generous and tender that He must reach 'outwards' from the Godhead in a ceaseless mission of love, to embrace, guide, console and teach all who will open their hearts at His touch. The Holy Spirit is always gathering in, purifying, and setting souls alight with His love: yet He is always One with the Source of all love: the Father - and with His Son, the eternal Word.

(Adapted from unpublished Teachings: T:3889 of 29.6.00 and 3899 of 1.7.00)

The Father reaches out in love to His Beloved Son;
and that 'Reaching-out-in-love' is the Holy Spirit.
(OIL-S:3889)

135

IN HIS PRESENCE.

What a marvel it is, that God has revealed Himself to us and has sent His Son to us. Christ came down to earth, at the time when He was conceived by the Holy Spirit in the womb of the Virgin Mary; and today, through the work of that same Spirit, Christ remains close to us. He is present in the assembly of the Faithful, and in the person of the priest, and in the Word of God: in Sacred Scripture; and He is also with us through His sacramental Presence - His Sacred Body and Blood, with His soul and Divinity: His 'Real Presence'. Christ is with us 'whole and entire' (CCC 1377) in the sacred species, both on the altar during the Mass, and in the tabernacle of each of our Catholic churches; and He delights in the love shown by all who come before Him in admiration and trust. He knows that His true friends recognise and welcome His Presence in church. They never treat a church as if it were a worldly place. They know that in stepping over the threshold, they have arrived at the 'edge' of Heaven.

We don't usually see Christ in prayer, or see His glory shine out from the tabernacle; but we know that He is now the triumphant Redeemer Who reigns in Heaven in glory, which is the glory, also, of the Father and of the Holy Spirit; and although it's true that we no longer take off our shoes in the Sacred Presence, because we're adopted children of God - temples of the Holy Spirit - we should always approach Christ with profound love and reverence. Whenever we honour the sacramental Presence of Christ - the living God Who is One with the Father and the Holy Spirit - we can be made joyful and at peace. We can shake off, for a while, some of the turmoil of everyday life in the world. By our glad yet reverent bearing in God's 'house of prayer' we can encourage other people to be reverent and so to practise the ways of Heaven. If we love God, we long to enter the City of the living God, to be close to Him eternally, and to celebrate, forever, there 'where the millions of Angels … have gathered for a festival' (Heb 12:22); and by adoring Christ in church, as if in Heaven's ante-chamber, we can prepare for the moment of our death.

(Adapted from an unpublished Teaching: of T:3915 of 13.7.00)

Before Christ, at the tabernacle, we are in the presence
of the living God, whose Triune glory fills the church.
(OIL-S:3915)

THE BURNING LOVE OF GOD

None of us knows what Heaven looks like. None of us has seen the Father's face. We cannot imagine the 'white-hot' love we shall meet in Heaven; but there, at the heart of the Three-in-One Whom we have worshipped in our earthly 'darkness', we can find answers to some of our questions, as well as the fulfilment for which we were made.

The image on the opposite page illustrates the fact that the Three Divine Persons - represented as three triangles - are distinct yet united. At the centre of the first triangle is a glowing fire, which is like white-hot molten lava. That fire extends through the centre of the other triangles, and signifies the Divine love at the heart of the Godhead: the pure, 'white-hot,' perfect love which God is: love which causes Christ to come amongst us at each celebration of the Mass, and to remain amongst us through His sacramental Presence in the tabernacle. This white-hot love makes each sanctuary of our churches resemble a furnace: an area which is full of a fire of love which is blazing fiercely, as it pours out graces from the Godhead.

We need only place ourselves before this fire, in trust and gratitude, in order to benefit. We can allow Christ to change our hearts. He can prepare us for Heaven, and for our meeting with the Father. Each of us has received existence from the Father - so we shall all meet Him, in the end; and that fiery life and light will be unbearable for those who have shunned His presence and spurned His holy laws; yet all who love Him will enjoy that an astonishing love which conveys healing, sweetness and peace, with a consoling presence - and with the promise that that blissful union shall never change. It will continue, blissful, forever: in the eternal 'Day' of Heaven. Divine love will be experienced, after our necessary purifications - whether we undergo these in everyday life or after our death - as unending, unutterable bliss and glory, and sweetness and peace.

(Adapted from *Teachings in Prayer Volume Four*, T:2143 of 23.2.97 and from an unpublished Teaching: T:4168, of 8.11.00).

*The pure, perfect love at the heart of the Holy Trinity
is like molten lava: white-hot, and purifying.
(OIL-S:4168)*

SHARING THEIR LIFE.

When a privileged and happy soul on earth is sharing, minute by minute, in the very life of the Godhead, through the Father's love and the merits of Christ the Son Who died for her, she can see how marvellously each of the Three Divine Persons sustains and strengthens her bond with Himself and also leads her to the Others. It's as though she has stepped onto a never-motionless wheel of joy and love, in which each of the Three Persons is tenderly 'at work' for her benefit and her enjoyment. The soul's rise into the heights, by God's Will and her co-operation, can be described thus: as if clockwise, from the foot of the image opposite. The Holy Spirit helps the soul 'into' the life of grace by directing her to a safe means of rising upwards, so that she can meet Christ - at the left - Who can help and heal her in the sacraments. Christ teaches the soul to turn to the Father - at the top - in confident prayer. The Father, by Providential means, leads the soul to rely on the Holy Spirit for daily guidance - as she listens to the Spirit's wordless promptings in prayer and also listens to the Church which is guided by Him; yet the work of the Three Persons has not ended. It's as if the wheel keeps turning.

The Holy Spirit turns the soul's attention always towards Christ, so that she will learn to imitate her Saviour. Christ brings the soul eventually to meet the Father, when the soul is truly 'one' with Christ in love and in knowledge. The Father guides the soul to notice the very 'workings' of the Holy Spirit within herself. The Holy Spirit steers the soul ever more firmly towards Christ in every situation, so that by meeting Christ in the sacraments and in prayer that soul will grow ever more fervent in love for God and for her neighbour. Weekly, or daily, through the Holy Eucharist, Christ is changing and purifying this soul so that, transformed, she can meet the Father one day in glory; and then she can stay forever with Him Who is her Origin, Goal and true home - with Christ her Saviour and the Holy Spirit, and with the Saints and the Holy Angels who, like her, have freely chosen to put God at the very centre of their lives.

(Adapted from an unpublished Teaching: T:4174 of 13.11.00)

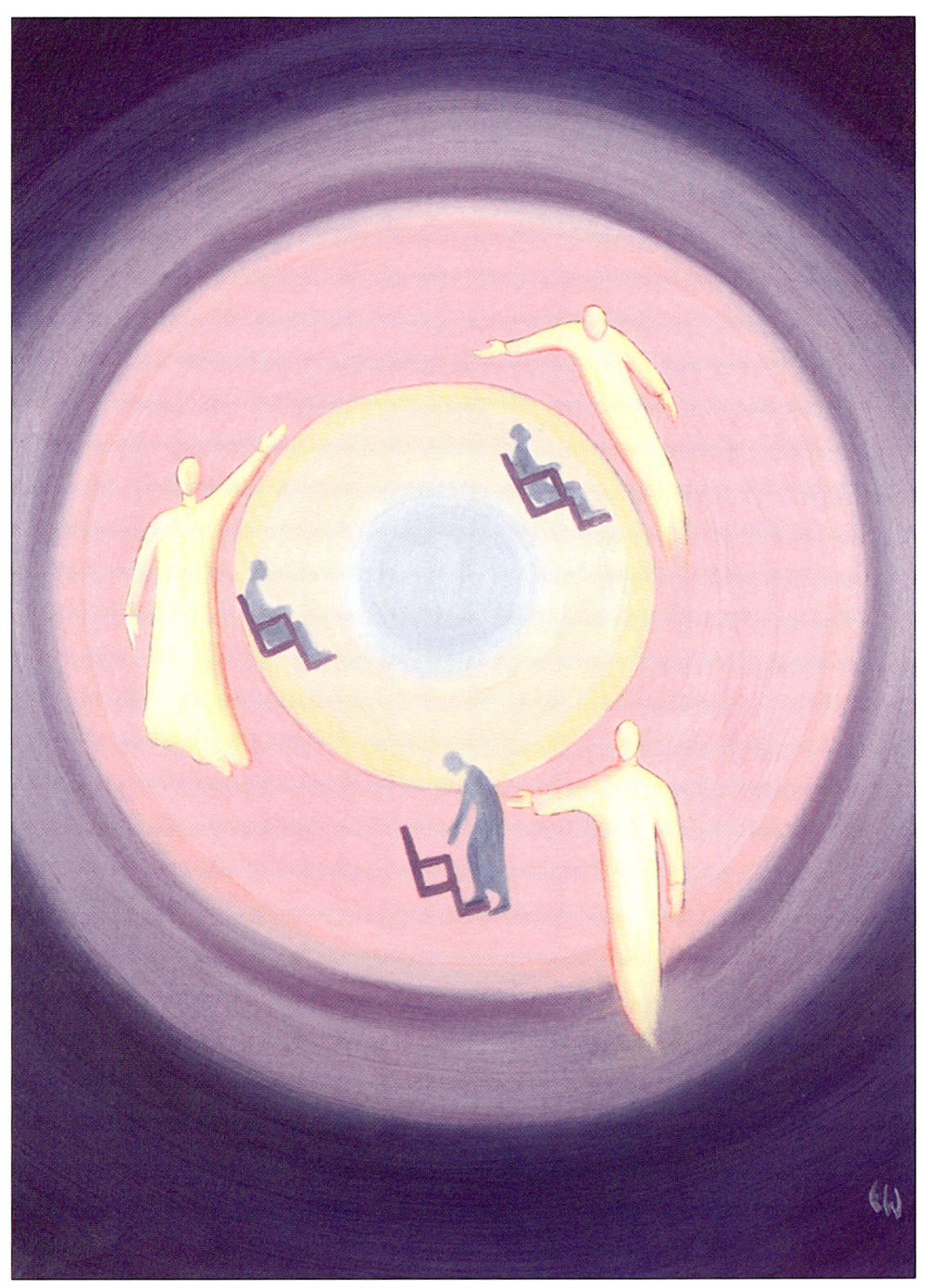

*Life 'in' God is like a never-motionless process of loving
guidance and assistance by the Three Divine Persons.*
(OIL-S:4174)

THREE PERSONS: ONE LOVE

While we still remain in earthly life, we can find God, no matter where we are. We can reach Him in a deserted part of the world or on the crowded pavements, in the dark void of our wounded heart or in the sunlight of our moments of fulfilment. He is never absent from us, but is always prompting us to pray. He always gazes lovingly upon us, ready to share His life and love with us, if only we'll open the 'door' of our souls.

Perhaps we like to chatter - friend to Friend - with Christ our Saviour. Perhaps we delight in offering reverent words of praise, or whispered endearments, to our Father in Heaven; or perhaps we call out, frequently, for the help of the Holy Spirit. Yet none of us, in pondering the glory of God's inner life, must forget the unity of the Godhead.

The painting gives a reminder that when we pray to one Divine Person we pray to the one, Triune God: whether we pray to the Father, the Son, or the Holy Spirit. There are not three Gods, but only One, in Whom are Three Divine Persons Who are distinct but united; and so, whenever we speak to Christ in prayer, we address, at the same time, the Father and the Holy Spirit. When we speak to the Father, we also address Christ and the Spirit; and when we speak to the Holy Spirit, we address, at the same time, the Father, and Christ His Son. Three Persons hear us: Three Divine Persons Who are gazing upon us with Infinite love and compassion.

We have good reason, however, to be faithful to the patterns of prayer which are treasured in the Church. Although we can pray to the Father or to the Son or to the Holy Spirit, it was Christ the Son - our Saviour - Who, during His life on earth, taught us to pray to the Father in His (Christ's) Name, in the power of the Holy Spirit; and so Christ's Church, for centuries, has formed and developed our patterns of Christian prayer in accordance with Christ's wishes.

(Adapted from an unpublished Teaching: T:4237 of 20.12.00)

Whoever prays to the Father, Son or Holy Spirit, prays to
the One, eternal God Who is undivided and unchanging.
(OIL-S:4237)

ONE ETERNAL OFFERING

Through and with Christ, we hope to enter the Godhead: to know and to enjoy God's Triune love, which is beyond our comprehension; yet we have learned about Christ's loving and eternal self-offering to the Father, in the Spirit. It is an offering to which we unite ourselves as it is shown out, on earth, in the Holy Sacrifice of the Mass. There is no greater act of worship on earth than the Mass; and the reason why the praise which is offered in the Mass is so powerful and exalted is that it is Christ's own praise, offered from our midst. At every Mass we participate more fully than at any other time in the eternal act of praise and love which takes place within the Godhead: within the 'heart' of the Holy Trinity. It's as though the Mass is the 'moment' at which we can leap most surely into Christ's perpetual loving prayer to the Father, in the Spirit, which takes place in Eternity; and if we look back for a moment to Christ's life on earth, and to the reason why Christ instituted the Holy Eucharist, we'll see that when He was doing His Father's Will on earth, whatever the cost, Christ was living out in the flesh, for our sakes, the very self-giving love which He has shown towards the Father from all Eternity.

He showed out that love by loving His Father's Will even when this led Him through an unjust trial, to the Cross; and so whoever makes himself one with Christ today in the living memorial of the Cross, by sincere participation in the Mass, is also one with Christ in His eternal self-offering in the inner life of the Holy Trinity. The image shows how everything God does is one great act of love. We can 'see' God's love for God, in God, in Eternity: the unending love of Three Divine Persons, which caused Christ to descend to earth to draw other people into the life and love of the Godhead. That same love is now made ours to offer to the Father through the Holy Eucharist. As we gather with our priest, by whose hands we offer Christ's sacrifice to the Father, in the Spirit, we offer a love and homage worthy of the Father. We increase our union with Him Who is love's Origin and source; and we have a foretaste of Heaven's joy.

(Based on an unpublished Teaching: T:4270 of 9.1.01)

When we are present to Christ's sacrifice of the altar, we
are present to His eternal self-offering in perfect love.
(OIL-S:4270)

145

IN THE TRANSFORMING UNION.

No human being can find words eloquent enough to praise the Holy Trinity in a manner which is worthy of the Divine glory. No words of ours are adequate to express thanks to the Three Divine Persons for Their goodness to us. If we belong to Christ, however, we know that He 'belongs' to us. We can count on His love; and in our bond of love with Him we have Him as our perfect Word of praise of the Father's glory, our perfect sacrifice to offer: the one who is like ourselves, though 'he is without sin' (Heb 3:15).

Someone who has been brought into the very life and heart of the Holy Trinity through ardent co-operation with Divine love, and through the purifying 'work' of prayer and penance and loving adherence to God's Will, with a sincere love for her neighbour, can picture herself as having a part in the wonderful 'web' of loving relationships within the Holy Trinity. She can rejoice in knowing that she is one with Each Divine Person, as Each pours out His Love towards those Others, within the Godhead.

The fortunate soul who has been brought, in a known way, into the Holy Trinity, in the transforming union, can say: "Since I belong wholly to God, through Christ, in the Spirit, I can be confident that I am one with the Holy Spirit in His eternal reaching-out in love, with Christ, to the Father. I am one with the Father in His eternal reaching-out to His Son, in the love of the Holy Spirit: and I am one with Christ in His eternal love for the Father, in the Spirit." To have arrived at this happy state, however, is not to have reached the end of the spiritual journey. It will end only at death, when the soul who has remained faithful right to the end of earthly life can at last enter Heaven; yet the enjoyment of God's friendship in the heights of prayer, in earthly life, can be seen as a fulfilment of the promises in which the soul believed when she first responded to God's invitation to become one with Him in love, and in prayer, and in work.

(Adapted from an unpublished Teaching, T:4299 of 27.1.01)

Whoever has been brought into the life and work of the Holy Trinity is
one with each Divine Person as each pours out love to the Others.
(OIL-S:4299)

147

IN PERPETUAL EXULTATION.

God the Holy Trinity is alive and active. The Godhead can be pictured as being like a great river of love - a triple ring of light and glory - which flows in Eternity in perpetual exaltation and delight, as the Three Divine Persons hold within Their life and love all who have become Their children, have persevered in love, and have been made worthy to enter Their embrace. Happy souls who have left behind the transient joys of earth have found, in the interior of the Godhead, a place of unending delight: an unmatched sweetness and an unparalled beauty. There, at God's heart, are vistas greater and more astounding than can be seen in a thousand universes. God's love is like balm to a wounded heart. His pure light delights those who have loved truth and beauty. Even during life on earth, however, we can enter this 'world' and this embrace, if we love God and live in a state of grace, and take part in the Holy Sacrifice. In meeting Christ, we meet the Father and the Holy Spirit. Even if nothing is seen, felt, touched or heard, we are thoroughly 'in touch' with God.

Our Communion in God, 'in' Christ, resembles God's own inner communion. It resembles the love of God for God, 'in' God: love which is flowing in the heart of God, in Eternity, in utter purity, majesty and simplicity.

That simple and everlasting love in Heaven is a three-fold love of Father, Son and Holy Spirit; and whenever we touch our Heavenly Father and enter His life, through Jesus, in the Holy Communion which is ours, on earth, we share the Father's life. The love is the same love. The Persons are the same, yet we are now drawn in by adoption. The moment is the same, since love has no end or beginning. The bliss is the same bliss, though it is muted, in our earthly life, lest we be destroyed by such unutterable joy; and, because of these things, we can say: "Heaven is here - even in our earthly life! In our Holy Communion, we 'taste' Heaven, in Christ."

Text adapted from unpublished Teachings: T:4315 of 5.2.01, T:4355 of 25.2.01, and T:1199 of 5.2.01.)

148

The Holy Trinity is alive in Eternity, like a triple ring of light
and glory, living in perpetual exultation and delight.
(OIL-S:4315)

WITH A THANKFUL HEART.

Christ is 'the radiant light of God's glory' (Heb 1:2). He has revealed the Father to us and has sent His Spirit to our hearts; and now He dwells amongst us through His sacramental Presence; and He looks with unutterable delight at each true friend of His who believes in Him, loves Him, and tries to serve Him with a sincere heart. With Christ, we can do worthwhile work: the lonely, and the sick and suffering, just as much as the able and the scholarly. Christ acts in His Church in every generation to bring hope to Mankind; so His Spirit urges some people to be willing workers who care for the sick, the poor or the homeless. Other people share the good news about the forgiveness of sins, and the hope of Heaven, by teaching the young, and by encouraging everyone to strive for holiness. Certain men - the Clergy - have been chosen by Christ to speak with authority. The Pope and the other Bishops, with the priests under their authority all united in faith, speak on Christ's behalf. Some people, by accepting sufferings, do a special part of Christ's work within the Church. Even if we cannot teach, care, or preach, we can 'live,' in our bodies, as Christ lived in His Passion. Through His merits, we can make reparation for sin, and draw down His grace upon other people. So each of us has a special role, whether hidden or well-recognised.

Truly, Christ is at work in the world through us, as we do His work of care, of teaching, of preaching and ruling, or of suffering and redeeming; and we can please Christ by kneeling before the sanctuary each day, to thank Him for our way of life. Clergy and laity can say, with thankful heart: "Lord: I praise and thank You for the honour You show me in using me to do Your work;" and whoever perseveres in faith, hope and love will be able to approach with joy, one day, the 'edge of Heaven', where Jesus stands with His holy Mother, in the presence of the Saints and the Angels. Each happy soul will be welcomed into the beauty of the Kingdom, to be with Christ forever, to enjoy the embrace of the Holy Spirit - and to see the Father's face.

(Text adapted from *Teachings-in-prayer Volume One*, T:1099 of 16.4.92, and also from an unpublished teaching, T:4384 of 10.3.01)

We honour God whenever we thank Him for
allowing us to do His work on earth.
(OIL-S:4384)

"Set me like a seal on your heart,
like a seal on your arm.
For love is strong as Death,
jealousy relentless as Sheol.
The flash of it is a flash of fire,
a flame of Yahweh himself.
Love no flood can quench,
no torrents drown."

(The Song of Songs: 8:6-7)

APPENDIX ONE

THE FATHER'S LOVE

We cannot see God, Whose Triune Glory has been
revealed to us through Christ: yet we can rejoice in
His infinite love for His creatures and admire every '
facet' of the Godhead.

I offer these few excerpts from His 'teachings', in
order to reveal some of the things He has shown me
in prayer, about His Divine nature.

In order to share His swift and soundless teachings
I have had to 'translate' them into human
language. Each of these teachings, however,
was given to me on a specific occasion, in prayer,
to increase my understanding of
the very things we've already learned through Christ
and the Church, for example, about the astonishing
'admixture,' in God, of majesty and tenderness, of
power and gentleness, purity and infinite compassion.

For further information about such teachings, please
see the Preface I've written for each volume of
'Teachings in Prayer,' published by
Radiant Light.

THE FATHER'S LOVE

A LOVING UNION
(from T:1941 of 23.6.96)

A JOYFUL MEETING.

Listen, My child;
"It is I",
your Father,
Who am reaching out to touch you,
because of My great love for you,
and your great love for Me.
I Who am love am the Lord of all things:
worthy of your daily sacrifices,
as you, with contrite heart,
make every effort to please Me
and to be fit for Heaven.
I assure you, My beloved,
that your surrender of your own wishes
has been wholly worthwhile.
I cannot fail to reward you.
You can be certain, therefore,
that through your union with Christ, My Son,
and through the help of His holy mother, Mary,
you have been well-prepared
for our joyful meeting.

It is true that I live far above you
in Heaven's splendour.
You can see that I dwell in the heights of glory;
yet here I am, My child, gazing upon you,
showing you the height and depth of our loving union;
and since you belong to Christ
there is no need for you to search for Me.

You can meet Me within your soul, in prayer,
as if in a tabernacle or a tent.

THE SOURCE OF LOVE.

Don't be afraid.
Truly,
it is I, your Heavenly Father
Who now reach out to touch you:
reaching out from Heaven's glory
to touch you with love!

As you can see
- in the fleeting image which is My gift to you -
it is through the outstretched 'hand'
of My Holy Spirit
that I bring My light and joy to you
in a moment of prayer.

Recognise My touch!
You and I are already united
in My Spirit's power,
through My Son, your Saviour,
and through your trusting prayer.
Have confidence in our friendship.
It is through our union and communion
that I can share My life with you, further,
bringing you greater joy,
and teaching you more about My nature:
about the love which is gentle
yet immensely powerful.
Treasure the knowledge
which you can 'see' in Me, today.

SPIRITUAL JOY.

Gaze towards the brightness of My glory

in contemplation.
Gaze, with the 'eyes' of your soul.
Look beyond all earthly things
- then beyond all images -
as My Holy Spirit brings you upwards
close to the furnace of love which is shining
at the heart of My life.
It is thus, through My invitation,
and through My light and power, in prayer,
that you can begin to fathom My nature,
which is love:
Divine love, in its beauty and perfection.

A SWEET LOVE.

Truly,
I am love,
and therefore
I am the Source
of all true love.
I am the cause
of your constant spiritual joy.
I am the light
which now illumines your heart and soul.
I am the bliss
at the heart of all true and holy love
in its bright, fiery joy and exhilaration.
I am the burning love
which warms and wounds the hearts
of all who love truth, goodness and beauty.
I am the sweet love
which binds together all true friends,
first, amidst the joys and trials of earthly life,
and then eternally: in Heaven's glory.

I am also a tender love.
I gaze upon you, now and always,
in the very way in which you gazed

- weeping for joy -
upon your new-born child.

THE ETERNAL PRIZE.

I am Divine love:
unchanging yet active: warm and effective.
I am the treasure
found by all who meet true love, on earth;
yet
you can say, of Me,
Who am bliss and light and love, unending,
that I am the eternal prize
of all who put their trust in Me
- even denying themselves love
in My service,
because of their love for Me -
and who remain faithful.
Heartache and pain are surrendered
by all who enter the heart of Heaven
for the marriage-feast.

THE BRIGHT FLAME.

Don't be afraid, My child.
Here I am: your Father, enlightening your soul.
I am the bright flame
at the heart of your prayer;
indeed,
I am the fire
at the heart of every moment
of true loving union and communion: whether
between ourselves,
or between you who are My children ...

THE SOURCE OF WISDOM.

Delight in My gifts.
I am the Source
of all wisdom.
I am the Giver
of all true peace;
furthermore,
it is I Who draw you to Heaven
- through Christ, and your prayer -
unveiling each stage of your way
on this spiritual journey.
Truly,
I am your guide;
and it is I who inspire you
to please Me.

PARADISE.

I am the Origin
of your longing to be holy.
I am the Father
of Christ the Beloved, in Whose name you pray.
I am the Love
- pure, perfect, unending, fiery and tender -
for which your soul is yearning.
I am the Goal
on your journey to Heaven,
as you follow the way of My Son.
I am the Home
in which you can shelter forever.
I am the Paradise
in which is found the perfect fulfilment
of every good longing,
with unending bliss for the human heart and mind
and body and soul.

It is my eternal wish, My child,

to see you joyful
eternally:
and to claim you as My own;
yet it is I, your God, Who now invite you
to claim and capture Me.

GREATER UNION.

Consider the benefits of even greater union.
What can you gain
but infinite bliss, and Heaven's gifts?
Believe in My love!
Cloaked in the darkness of contemplation,
you soul is like a tent
- or a tabernacle -
where I, your Father, meet you and greet you.
Here I am: love Himself,
to teach you.

Truly,
you are My precious child.
It was I who created you.
I Myself have led you towards love, purity and holiness;
and now, in this 'custody' and communion
I make no demands
but rather,
I make Myself 'prisoner' to your desire
as your every prayer is granted!

So great is My love,
and so tender My care for you,
that now I cherish your every wish,
whether expressed or unspoken.
Who is like Me, your God?
Who, therefore, can rival
My wooing of your soul?
Whose love or gift, whose word or tenderness

can rival Mine?

EQUAL IN SELF-GIVING.

See how I act, in this custody and communion.
I, your Creator, relinquish My power!
You who once feared Me are now
wholly at rest,
overjoyed by My kindness:
touched to the heart to discover My plan,
which is that I, your God, serve you.
I comfort you,
My beloved.
Here, in our union,
we are equal in self-giving.
I am doing your will,
by granting your heart's desires.

Yours, now, is the joyful knowledge
that your every request is granted.
Now at last you realise
what is happening in our prayer,
in the bond of love,
and in the marriage of our hearts.
I, your Lord,
your beloved and all-holy Creator
now reveal to you
the astonishing result of our love.

I Who am love
- the All-Glorious, the All-Holy -
am now 'captive' to you
My creature.

THE TRUE HOMELAND
(from T:2169 of 23.3.97)

LIVING IN GOD.

Dear child,
I delight in your prayers of gratitude
for Christ My Son, for life and faith,
and for every blessing.
I delight in your longing to know Me.
I delight in your delight in Me
even as you seek further understanding.
Truly,
I am drawing you into My life even further,
because I am good, and also
because you have accepted My invitation.
I am the 'medium' in which you live and pray
as you live 'in God':
as you soar within My being,
in contemplation.
Delight in our union.
Be at peace in My love.

A TORRENT OF LIGHT AND JOY.

Truly,
I am the heart
from which you were born.
I am He
in Whom you dwell, in friendship.
I am the homeland
in which you can move freely.
I am the infinite torrent of light and joy
in which you soar, praying.

I am the goal
of your yearning heart.
I am the destination
at which, through our union, you already arrive.
I am the love
in which you are held, in My embrace.
I am the 'playground'
for you, My children,
as you search, now enraptured ,
in silent prayer,
in the vast, soaring heights of My Infinite love,
in safety.

UNRIVALLED JOYS
(from T:2180 of 5.4.97)

LOVE'S FULL EXTENT.

Little child:
My love for you is so great
that I cannot yet reveal to you
the full extent of its majesty and beauty,
lest you hesitate on your journey,
overwhelmed by love's intensity,
and afraid.

I delight in your acts of faith in My love.
I delight in seeing you prayerful and joyful
and also
seeing you use time so well,
even in sickness,
and seeing you offer a new surrender
to My wishes.

Believe this, My child:

My love for you is so genuine, powerful and unstoppable
that I am reaching out all the time
to draw you further into My embrace,
and further into my heart.

GOOD NEWS.

Share with others
- and with the whole world, through your work -
the truth about My love:
about Divine love for weak persons.

Reassure others
that nothing can compare with the gifts
which I, your Father, so tenderly bestow.

Reassure My people
that
no earthly love
- no experience of natural happiness,
no romance,
no worldly fulfilment,
no joyful and satisfying use
of mind, body, memory or imagination,
nor any human joy -
can rival Heaven's joys.

Nothing can surpass the intensity
of the utter bliss and glory
which are My gifts
- sometimes even during earthly life -
to
My true friends.

LAVISH GIFTS.

Never forget,
beloved child:
My nature is love.
Everything which comes from Me
springs from love;
so there is no need for you to worry.

Consider My nature, then ask yourself:
why be surprised
at My lavish distribution of gifts?
Why be overcome
at the sight of your unworthiness,
when you are rightly convinced that I love you?
I delight in your gratitude
for everything good.
Continue to trust in Me
and in My plans.

JOY AND GLORY.

Consider your state of soul
on this 'Feast of the Holy Trinity'
as you adore Us:
one God,
yet
three Persons,
and as you offer your life, once more,
in Our service,

The joy and glory within your soul are gifts from Me,
but also serve as means of instruction
about the Godhead:
about My life.
Joy and glory are the 'climate'
enjoyed by all who live 'in' Me,
in true union.
I am wholly occupied
with love.

THE 'WORK' OF HEAVEN.

We Three Persons
are 'occupied'
in a ceaseless, unbroken, and blissful
mutual giving and receiving of perfect love,
'in' joy and glory;
and whoever consents to Our love and action
is drawn into Our heart.
It is as though, in prayer, you are leaping, joyfully
- even now , in earthly life -
into the bliss and glory
of the Divine life of the Holy Trinity:
into the heart of one God:
eternal joy.

WITHOUT WORDS
(from T:2766 of 22.8.98)

WRAPPED IN GLORY.

My child,
I have brought you so close to Me
that I have led you at last, to a special union,
to become radiant with My light,

and to remain close to My heart.

You have become 'one will' with Me;
and in our pure communication
- as if Mind to mind, in perfect silence -
I rarely 'pierce' your soul with knowledge,
as in earlier days;
rather,
I Myself wrap you in glory,
suffuse your heart with joy
and 'talk' to you without words.

INTO HIS PRESENCE
(from T:2773 of 26.8.98)

IN LOVE AND ADMIRATION.

I delight in your delight,
My child,
as you speak to Me in admiration,
as you think about My love for you,
as you gaze upon My majesty and glory,
as you delight in every aspect of My nature,
as you long to make known the Good News
about your hope of salvation,
and as you long to see other people
turn towards Me with trusting hearts
to express their gratitude and praise.

It is because you love Me
and you delight in Me
that I now increase your understanding
of the way in which I act.
Such understanding can bring greater joy
to your already-joyful and devoted heart.

ONE ACT.

Listen to these words, My child,
about the 'essence' of My nature:
All that I do is one act.
Examine this sequence, My child,
as I speak of Mankind and its fall.
See how simple I am,
in the following sense.

First, I created you, My children;
and you disobeyed me.
You sinned.
Then I sent down Christ My Son
Who shed His blood for you,
and died for you.
I drew up a plant from the earth:
a vine from the earth once 'watered'
by Christ's blood.
I inspired you to cultivate these plants:
vines strong and fruitful;
and thus I gave you wine
for your use and pleasure;
and it is I, My child
- by My powerful work, through the Spirit -
who now change that wine
into the Precious Blood of Christ
My only Son;
and through this marvellous means
I nourish your souls.
I transform you.
I make you like Christ.

THROUGH LIFE AND DEATH.

Now you can see how I draw you
to Myself, through Christ:
"in, with, and through Him"

towards Me,
as if full-circle, in your life-span.

It's as if you 'move' out from Me
- 'out' from My mind -
to move through conception, birth and life,
to be nourished and transformed by My power
in the sacraments,
and then to move, through death,
'full-circle' into My presence.

CHRIST'S LOVING ACT
(from T:2782 of 4.9.98)

AN ACT OF LOVE.

In speaking of the Holy Eucharist,
go to the heart of it.
Tell these enquirers
that the Holy Sacrifice of the Mass
- the Holy Eucharist -
is an act of love.
Help them to understand
that I, Who created you,
love you with an infinite love.
*I have reached down to you all
in your desperate need.*
I gave My only Son to be born on earth
and to live amongst you.
I gave Him to die for you;
and then I raised Him up to a new life
in which you can share one day
in bliss and glory
if you put your trust in Him,
allow Him to transform you,

and remain faithful to the end.

THE SAME SACRIFICE.

Explain, My child,
about the holy sacrifice of the Cross:
It was the loving act by which
Christ reconciled Mankind to Me, His Father;
and that same sacrifice of Calvary
is re-presented before you, on the altar,
somewhere in the world, daily or hourly.
It is a loving act.

It is Christ's loving act
by which supreme homage is offered
- in the Spirit -
to Me, His beloved Father,
and by which salvation is offered, today,
to all who put their trust in Him,
their Redeemer and friend.

FAR-AWAY DEPTHS
(from T:2859 of 21.11.98)

A GLORIOUS PANORAMA.

Here I am, My child,
to give you a glimpse of My beauty:
though not of My face,
nor of the 'heart' of the Godhead,
but to give you a closer look
at My radiant glory
as it sweeps past you for a moment,
in accordance with My Will.
This fast-moving panorama

is My brief and blessed gift to you:
to the eyes of your soul, in prayer.
It is a gift made possible
only through My Will, your faith,
and our bond of pure charity.

A BEAUTIFUL PRESENCE.

Here is a distant vision of light
wholly surrounded by pure radiance;
and here within, you can find
grace and power and motion,
as you gaze into far-away depths
and glance upon bright, near-by marvels.
Truly, I am here.
I am a purposeful and beautiful presence
now hidden from you
within a moving image.

Even as I wordlessly 'speak' to you
I choose to conceal Myself, My child,
within a formless presentation
of unfocussed beauty;
yet I want you to know
that every aspect of true beauty
is found in Me in Heaven:
both in the depths of Divine life
and in the heights of My unveiled glory.

THE SOURCE OF GLORY.

Rejoice in this gift, today.
Treasure this brief and blessed taste
- through a vision in prayer -
of My bright but intangible beauty.
All the beauty of the earth and the heavens
is found in Me,

since I am the Origin
of everything beautiful on earth
and I am the Source and heart
of Heaven's glory.
What you are seeing in this moment
is something inexpressible
yet very near to you:
something intangible
yet close to your heart.
Who could find words
to describe it?

A RADIANT VISION.

I am your God
Who made you, and love you.
Here I am, to satisfy
your thirst for knowledge
about Me;
yet My spiritual beauty is so great
that it cannot be captured in words.
If you could speak about Me
to other people,
- if you could offer a few inadequate phrases -
you could say, of My beauty,
which is here expressed, yet half-hidden
in a glorious and radiant vision:
that it has the power and the grace
of the curve of a huge wave
on the vast ocean;
yet it possesses the joy and freedom
of the leaping-up of a fine young stallion.
It is something gentle and spiritual
which has the softness and delicate grandeur
of those huge, bright, billowing clouds
- tinged with sunlight -
which so enchant you

after a storm.
It is something lively yet invisible:
all-at-once familiar and yet sublime.

THE HOPE OF HEAVEN.

I am showing you such glimpses, My child,
because of My love for you,
and because of your love for Me:
love which you marvellously express
in sincere and ardent prayer.

You have faith, hope and love;
and My desire, in showing this sight,
is to see your hope grow even stronger.
Hope for Heaven.
Hold fast to the knowledge
that I am all-beautiful and all-holy,
and that you can find, within My life,
sights which will evoke in your soul
joy, astonishment and awe.

EVERY ASPECT OF BEAUTY.

Here in the Godhead,
in My light and life and glory,
all beauty is experienced,
in an ever-renewed presentation,
as an infinitely-wondrous showing-out
of every aspect of beauty.
Even today, in your prayer,
My beauty delights you,
though I must 'limit' your vision
because of My radiance and your frailty;
but I assure you that in Heaven,
at the end of your life on earth,
the joy which you will experience

on seeing My infinite beauty
will be blissful and unsurpassable;
and your joy will be perfected
by the knowledge that it will never end.

THREE -IN-ONE
(from T:2863 of 26.11.98)

THREE PERSONS: ONE GOD.

You honour Me by your love,
and by your heart-felt yearning
to be one in prayer, each day,
with My Son
and with His Body, the Church;
and that is why I remind you,
not to teach you what you know,
but rather, to encourage you,
that whenever you praise one of Us
- one of three Divine Persons -
you praise one God:
the Holy Trinity.

DISTINCT, YET UNDIVIDED.

Remember, always,
that whenever you praise Me, your Father,
you also honour Christ, and the Holy Spirit.
Whenever you praise Christ,
you also praise Myself, and the Holy Spirit;
and whenever you praise the Holy Spirit,
you also praise Christ My Son - and Myself.
Truly,
I now affirm what you have believed:
that I am one:

one God:
Three Persons Who are distinct,
yet Who share the same nature.
We are undivided:
eternally one.

THE GREATEST GRACES
(from T:2993 of 11.2.99)

FROM EXPERIENCE.

What a cause for celebration!
You have had confirmed,
from experience,
the truth in which you already believed:
the truth that I, your God,
Three-in-One,
look upon you
with infinite love.

THE GREATEST GRACES.

You have found
that no love is greater
than My love:
the love of your God and Father.
You have found
that no bliss is greater
than the bliss which is given
by the Holy Spirit
Who can suffuse body and soul
with Heavenly sweetness.
You have found
that no greater joy and glory are given
than the joy and glory

which are shared with you
in Holy Communion
by Jesus Christ, My Son;
and you have found
that He gives the greatest graces
to the most welcoming and devoted hearts.

EXPRESSIONS OF LOVE
(from T:3021 of 27.4.99)

AN ETERNAL OFFERING.

Here I am, My child,
to increase your understanding
of the offering which Christ has made to Me;
and by this, I mean
His self-offering to Me from all ages,
His self-offering, in death on Calvary,
His self-offering made today, in this church,
on the holy altar,
and His self-offering to Me
for all ages to come.
I want you to know
that His offering is not four-fold.
"It is one."

It is as though Christ has only
one perpetual and unchanging 'stance' of love
towards Me
in an offering which
- in your understanding -
seems to be demonstrated
at different times.

AT DIFFERENT TIMES.

Be happy, my child,
that you are present here, one with Christ,
as He holds out to Me
through His generous self-giving
an eternal and perfect offering of love
which you who live in time
'see' as offered at different times.
I know that you have pondered, for example,
four particular truths:
first, about Christ's love being expressed
in Eternity, before His Incarnation,
and then about His self-sacrifice
on Calvary, upon the Cross;
and also about His triumph,
when He greeted Me with infinite love
in His Resurrection and Ascension,
in His 'return' to Me, in Heaven;
and you have marvelled at the love He will show Me
for all ages to come.

ONE WITH CHRIST.

I want you to know
that so powerful and magnificent
and infinitely-tender towards Me
is Christ's eternal expression of love
that it's as though its fiery delight
burns like a wondrous majestic light
- without diminishing in strength -
from the altar in your church.
It reaches up high
as far as the infinite heights of Heaven;
and whenever you unite yourselves
to Christ, in the Mass,
you are one with Him

in His one, perpetual offering to Me
of His infinitely-great and holy love;
yet you can be one with Him, also,
in that very same offering
through a simple, loving intention,
at any time of the night or day.

BY A LOVING INTENTION.

Remember, My child,
what I once told you
about self-giving, and adoration.
Whenever you are joyful, or grateful to Me,
or contrite, or yearning to praise Me,
and so are yearning to be united to Christ
in His perpetual act of love for Me
you can indicate your loving intention
in a very simple way.
You can be one with Him
through a little movement of your willing heart.
If you wish to offer perfect praise to Me
you are not limited
to the Holy Sacrifice of the Mass.
By the simple 'glance' and consent
which I have explained to you
you are one with Christ
in the loving act
which He offers from all eternity,
one with Christ
in His loving self-offering of Calvary,
one with Christ
in His loving act
as it is represented on the altar,
and one with Christ
in His act of total self-giving
which has continued in Eternity
since His Ascension to glory.

FULL PARTICIPATION.

Share the Good News, My child.
Let Me make it plain
through you and your writings
that although it is the duty and privilege
of every 'child of God'
to participate fully in the Mass,
as requested by Christ
through His Church,
your praise need not be limited
to those times
when the Holy Sacrifice is offered
from your altar.
Christ's perfect praise is 'yours' to claim
at every moment of your life.

PERFECT PRAISE.

In union with Christ
you have only to whisper this thought
or wordlessly to express it:
"Here I am, Father:
one with Christ, in praising You,
in the Spirit;"
and you can be certain
that you are marvellously united to Christ
in His 'entire,' single act of praise:
praise which consists of
Christ's praise in eternity,
Christ's praise from the Cross,
Christ's praise at His Resurrection
and His Ascension into Heaven
and therefore, also,
Christ's praise from every altar in the world
where the whole paschal mystery
is re-presented.

IN ETERNITY.

Keep in mind, always,
and teach other people,
that all of Christ's praise
is one;
and it is yours to offer
if you are willing,
and if you belong to Christ
through your faith, hope and love.
Share the good news
that each one of you can be involved
in the very life and work and praise
of the Godhead:
in the life of the Three Divine Persons
of the Most Holy Trinity.
This is work in which you can share
in earthly life, as I have told you;
yet it is work
which you can continue in Eternity
in the company of the Saints.

VERY CLOSE TO US
(from T:3115 of 9.7.99)

IN EVERY THOUGHT.

Be joyful, My child,
even amidst your struggles and strivings.
In every thought of yours
about life or work or joys or problems,
or the delights of prayer
or the certainty of death,
hold fast, and hold joyfully
to the knowledge that I am close to you.

I am closer
than your own thoughts and emotions.
I am your loving Father;
and My 'ambition' for you
is to see you wholly fulfilled and joyful:
to see you 'immersed' eternally
in the joy and peace of Heaven.

THE SOURCE OF ALL GOOD
(from T:3226 of 26.9.99)

GIFTS OF THE SPIRIT.

All good things come from Me:
from the heart of the Holy Trinity;
so there's no need to worry, My child,
about your work.

Every good spiritual gift
stems from My Holy Spirit.
He gives wisdom and understanding.
He causes you to take delight
in whatever is genuinely good.
He prompts you to do what is good.
He now prompts you to describe
what I have just shown you
in our prayer.
Thus, you will bring towards completion
some of the good work
already begun at His bidding.

CROWNED AND ADORNED
(from T:3294 of 30.10.99)

ENJOYING GOD'S FRIENDSHIP.

Consider this, My child.
Reflect with wonder, upon these marvels:
that the soul who enjoys My friendship
and who perseveres in love and prayer
finds, in the end, to her astonishment,
that she is crowned and adorned
with spiritual jewels.
She is held in My peace.
She is suffused by Divine sweetness.
She is enlightened by the Holy Spirit.
She is bathed in My glory.
She is made warm-hearted by My graces.
She is lifted, powerfully,
above earthly pains and concerns.
She is loved, and she is held in love,
by Father, Son and Holy Spirit:
by the one, only God
Who has formed and created her
and Who, from love, has invited her
to share His Divine life.

A FIRE OF LOVE
(from T:3319 of 11.11.99)

INCOMPARABLE SWEETNESS.

I Who am Truth

have shown you the truth
about My Divine nature.
It is so radiantly pure and powerful
that whoever meets it unprepared
would be frightened or harmed
by such contact;
yet you have also learned,
through prayer,
that there is no love to match Mine:
nor any tenderness or sweetness on earth
to match My sweetness and tenderness
towards you.

You have experienced the sweetness
of My nature
because you allowed Me
to purify and transform you, in Christ,
and to draw you into close friendship
in a bond of sweetness and love.

A GRADUAL REVELATION.

If you consider the frailty of human beings,
and if you consider My power and glory
you can see clearly
that, many centuries ago,
I revealed myself to My Chosen People
in the only possible way:
revealing Myself little by little
through gentle words and invitations
and then through mighty wonders,
in extraordinary signs
and in necessary warnings.
That is how I taught
all who would listen to Me
about the astonishing juxtaposition, in Me,
of tenderness and majesty.

It's as if I am like a mighty 'fire' of love
which blazes for mile upon mile
beyond a range of distant mountains.
My glory is lighting up the sky;
yet by this distance I protect frail creatures
who, were they to see Me as I am,
would be destroyed.

SHIELDED FROM DIVINE GLORY.

In order to come amongst frail human beings
- to teach you about Myself and about My plan -
I acted with caution and care.
In a particular time and place
I sent you My Son
to be born of a woman.
Jesus Christ is true God, made man.
Truly, He is my Son:
love incarnate : love embodied;
and whoever marvels
on seeing how the fire of love
came amongst you on earth
will marvel even more on realising
that those who met Jesus
were 'shielded' from His Divine glory
by His humanity:
except at His Transfiguration,
when the apostles were awestruck
on seeing that radiance revealed.
Whoever is astonished that I, your Creator,
have come to earth, through My Son,
to walk amongst My creatures
and have done so from no other motive
but infinite love
must marvel even more
at the knowledge of Christ's generosity.
He not only lived earthly life for you

but, for your sakes,
endured earthly torment, even enduring
death on a cross.

TRUE BELIEVERS.

What can any of you do, in gratitude,
if you are indeed a true believer,
except honour and serve My Son
Who leads you towards the Heavenly home
where He awaits you, in glory?
What can you do, to show gladness,
except speak gladly about Him,
share your joy in His friendship,
and work with all your power
to spread the good news of His love?

Everything Christ did in His earthly life
showed out My love, and My nature;
yet what a cause for gratitude, My child,
in your own life on earth:
that you didn't remain
always puzzled and ignorant
but found out the truth about Christ,
the truth about the Godhead,
the truth about My plan for Mankind,
and the truth about Christ's Holy Catholic Church.

IN MAJESTY AND POWER
(from T:3939 of 21.7.00)

A REVELATION.

My child,
you have a grateful heart.

186

You long to know Me better.
You have just told Me
that You long to see Me.
That's why I now reveal to you
several aspects of My nature.

FAR ABOVE.

In My Divine life
I am further 'above' you all
than the most towering feature
of an earthly landscape.
In My majesty and power
I am more imposing
than the greatest tidal wave
as it roars from the deep ocean.
In My justice
I am like a huge bird of prey:
silent and clear-sighted:
swift and perfect in my acts and intentions.
In My unchanging Will
I am like the steady and perpetual descent
of a vast waterfall in a forest.
In My judgements
I am like a cloud so high and dark
that it blots out the sun; yet
in My mercy
I am like the best and sweetest friend.
In My grace and beauty
I am like the leaping creature
of the great southern plains; and
in My love
I am like the most faithful and tender lover
who dazzles his beloved
with the gifts he brings
yet who moves her heart most deeply
by his sweetness,

and by his gentle care.

TRUE FRIENDSHIP
(from T:3293 of 29.10.99)

A SPECIAL LANGUAGE.

This is the marvel of true union:
This is our 'language', My child,
in our friendship.
This is our conversation
as day follows day:
I 'speak' without sound.
I warm your heart without fire.
I hold you without touching.
I reassure you without words.
I embrace you without end
unless, solely to please Me,
you go 'away' from prayer
to do a little more of our work.

HIS OWN PRECIOUS CHILD
(from T:3968 of 7.8.00)

LORD OF THE OCEANS.

Here I am, My child,
to console you,
and to reward you for your sincere prayer.
It is true that in speaking to Me
you address a God of majesty and power.
I am the only God:
God of the winds and gales and tidal waves:

Lord of the deep oceans.
Whenever You speak to Me
You address Him Whose power is seen
in the storms which sweep over the pathway
and cause the roads by the shore
to shake to their foundations;
yet if I am majesty and power
I am love, also.

A SPECIAL WELCOME.

I am Divine love:
a love so utterly loving and tender
that it's as if I am helpless
in the face of true love:
for example,
when I meet your love in prayer.

That's why I lay aside My grandeur
in order to greet you and welcome you,
as a good Father greets his precious child:
turning to you gently, always,
with wholehearted attention
and immeasurable delight.

WHO AND WHAT IS GOD?
(from T:4355 of 25.01.01)

WHO AND WHAT?

Here I am, My child,
responding to your question.
You believe in Me.
You love Me;
and you turned to Me in hope and trust

189

- in Christ, and through the Spirit -
to say: "I long to see You;"
and yet, burning to know Me better,
you asked:
"Who are You," and: "What are You?"
So here I am, to explain:
not with words,
but through My loving presence.

LOVE'S PRESENCE.

Truly,
here I am, for you:
as I give you, with great gentleness,
My very self:
as I reveal My nature to you,
as if to a child,
revealing it very gently,
stage by stage.

Here I am, for you
as spiritual sweetness
as I share the Heavenly bliss
which is love made 'palpable'.

Here I am, for you,
as I touch you
with a gentle Breath
which is life, undying.

Here I am, for you,
as I reveal Myself
as a pure fiery light
which is My eternal radiance.

Here I am, for you,
as I gently enfold you,

giving you the peace-of-soul
which is My embrace.

Here I am, for you,
as I share My life with you
by a suffusion of warmth
which is My holy presence
now being experienced
throughout your whole being.

Here I am, therefore,
to give a loving reminder
that every cell of your body
has been designed, created, given life,
and held in existence
by Me,
and that I delight in you,
and in your expressions of love.

INFINITE CHARITY.

Now you can see, child,
how I have shown you My nature.
I have shown you, not through words
but through self-giving love,
precisely Who and What I am.

Now I have made plain to you
something of My life in Eternity.
It is a life sweeter, warmer,
more loving and more wondrous
than anything you have imagined.
It is a life which consists of
Divine love:
unending, generous, and astonishing love:
a life of infinite charity and sweetness.

A JOURNEY INTO GOD
(from T:4372 of 2.3.01)

THROUGH CHRIST.

I have answered your prayer,
My child.
My Spirit is at work
in order to help you.
By His gift and power
He increases the joy within your soul.
He thus enables you to see
even more clearly
what gifts He has brought to your soul
through your union with Me
in Christ.
If you can 'see' His gifts My child,
you can describe them, to help other people.
I want you to write in detail, today,
about your consoling prayer.

THE SPIRIT'S TOUCH.

Remember:
you greeted Me with love;
then you praised and thanked Me
through Christ, in the Spirit,
for every blessing.
You prayed for the Clergy, and for the whole Church;
then you remained in My presence
in silence and contentment,
waiting for My Will to be revealed;
and so I reached out to you
to reward you for your trust.

I lifted up your soul
suddenly, gently.
I gave you joy
through My Spirit Who first gave you life;
and as you trusted in Him Who loves you
and surrendered to His Will
you allowed Him to teach you.
You enabled Him to show you
in an extraordinary manner
how He is at work in your life
and in your prayer.

You were touched by a Breath
but saw no face.
You were held in flight,
but felt no movement.
You felt a wind,
with no disturbance of the air.
You went on a journey,
yet with no vehicle.
You received a gift
which bore no label.
You knew a sweetness
which had no taste.
You were being held,
but in utter nothingness.
You were warmed,
yet by no visible fire.
You knew delight:
unexpected, indescribable, Divine;
and you knew joy, receiving it
as if by a sudden immersion in bliss;
and this is a joy which, if you are faithful,
can be yours without end,
here at My heart,
in Heaven.

APPENDIX TWO

DIAGRAMS

Since it is not always clear, in
the seventy-four paintings in this
book, which of the Three Divine Persons is
represented singly in an image, or - where
the Three are represented together - which
is the Father, or the Son or the Holy Spirit, I
have prepared the following pages of
diagrams, to make these things plain.

The images are not intended to be portraits of
the Three Divine Persons; rather, they are
a pictorial means, given in prayer, of
describing the life and work and love of the
Holy Trinity.

DIAGRAMS

OIL-S: 50
on page 3

THE FATHER

THE SON

THE
HOLY
SPIRIT

The soul

OIL-S: 65
on page 5

THE   THE
SON   HOLY
                  SPIRIT

The soul

THE
FATHER

OIL-S: 67
on page 7

THE FATHER
THE SON
THE HOLY SPIRIT

Saints   Saints

The Soul

OIL-S: 68B
on page 9

THE FATHER
THE SON
THE HOLY SPIRIT

The soul

OIL-S: 110
on page 11

THE FATHER

THE
HOLY
SPIRIT
                  THE
                  SON

The soul

OIL-S: 259
on page 13

THE
FATHER
THE
SON
THE
HOLY
SPIRIT

Saints   The soul

OIL-S: 290
on page 15

THE FATHER

THE SON

The soul
THE HOLY SPIRIT

OIL-S: 461
on page 17

THE FATHER

HOLY   THE
SPIRIT   SON

The soul

OIL-S: 481A
on page 19

THE FATHER
THE HOLY SPIRIT
THE SON

Saints

The soul

OIL-S: 493A
on page 21

THE FATHER

THE SON
Souls
THE HOLY SPIRIT

OIL-S: 535
on page 23

THE FATHER
THE HOLY SPIRIT

THE SON

Souls

OIL-S:546
on page 25

THE FATHER
THE HOLY SPIRIT
THE SON

The soul

OIL-S: 565
on page 27

The Soul

THE FATHER
THE SON
THE HOLY SPIRIT

Souls

OIL-S: 572
on page 29

THE
FATHER

THE
HOLY
SPIRIT

THE SON

Souls

OIL-S: 576
on page 31

THE FATHER
THE SON
THE HOLY SPIRIT

Souls

OIL-S: 588
on page 33

THE
FATHER

THE   THE
SON   HOLY
             SPIRIT

Souls

OIL-S: 811
on page 35

THE
SON

The
Priest

OIL-S: 1039C
on page 37

THE FATHER

THE   THE
SON   HOLY
             SPIRIT

The
Soul

OIL-S: 1197
on page 39

THE FATHER

THE
SON

THE HOLY SPIRIT

Souls

OIL-S:1244
on page 41

THE
FATHER

THE HOLY SPIRIT

THE
SON

The
Soul

OIL-S:1259
on page 43

THE
FATHER

THE HOLY SPIRIT

THE SON

The   The
Soul   Priest

OIL-S: 1320
on page 45

THE
SON

OIL-S: 1351C
on page 47

THE FATHER

THE HOLY SPIRIT
THE
SON

The
earth

OIL-S: 1366
on page 49

THE FATHER
THE SON
THE HOLY SPIRIT

The
Soul

OIL-S: 1385A
on page 51

THE FATHER

THE   The   THE
SON   Soul   HOLY
                                  SPIRIT

OIL-S: 1385B
on page 53

THE FATHER

THE   THE
SON   HOLY
                 SPIRIT

The Soul

OIL-S: 1396
on page 55

THE FATHER

The Soul

OIL-S: 1409
on page 57

```
        THE FATHER



        THE HOLY SPIRIT



Souls      THE      Souls
           SON
```

OIL-S:1439
on page 59

```
    THE FATHER


                    THE
                    HOLY
THE                 SPIRIT
SON
         The
         earth
```

OIL-S:1469A
on page 61

```
            THE
            FATHER
            THE
            SON
         The soul
            THE
         HOLY SPIRIT
```

OIL-S: 1476
on page 63

```
THE FATHER
THE HOLY SPIRIT
      THE
      SON


Souls
```

OIL-S: 1541
on page 65

```
        THE
        FATHER
        THE
        SON
        THE
     HOLY SPIRIT

      The soul
```

OIL-S: 1548
on page 67

```
        THE FATHER


                    THE
THE                 HOLY
SON                 SPIRIT


         The soul
```

OIL-S: 1588
on page 69

```
              The earth

         Souls

    THE
    SON
THE
FATHER
             THE
             HOLY
             SPIRIT
```

OIL-S: 1626
on page 71

```
     THE FATHER
     THE SON
  THE HOLY SPIRIT
```

OIL-S: 1632
on page 73

```
THE FATHER
THE HOLY SPIRIT
THE SON


      Souls
```

OIL-S: 1685B
on page 75

```
THE
FATHER

THE HOLY SPIRIT
          THE
          SON

        Souls
```

OIL-S: 1720
on page 77

```
            THE
            FATHER

    THE       THE
    SON       HOLY
              SPIRIT

    The
    earth
```

OIL-S: 1776A
on page 79

```
        THE FATHER

    THE HOLY SPIRIT


            THE
            SON

           Souls
```

OIL-S: 1794
on page 81

```
        THE
        FATHER

THE
SON
        The
        Soul
        THE
        HOLY SPIRIT
```

OIL-S: 1839
on page 83

```
THE FATHER


THE HOLY SPIRIT
The Priest
THE SON
```

OIL-S: 1913
on page 85

```
        THE
        FATHER
        THE
        SON
        THE
        HOLY SPIRIT
```

OIL-S: 1941
on page 87

```
        THE
        HOLY
        SPIRIT

The
Soul
```

OIL-S: 1978
on page 89

```
THE     THE     THE
SON   FATHER   HOLY
                SPIRIT
```

OIL-S: 2003B
on page 91

```
        THE FATHER

    THE HOLY SPIRIT

            THE
            SON


    The
    earth
```

OIL-S: 2138
on page 93

THE SON

The priest

OIL-S: 2169
on page 95

THE
FATHER
THE
SON
THE
HOLY
SPIRIT

The soul

OIL-S: 2221
on page 97

THE
FATHER

THE
HOLY
SPIRIT
THE
SON   The
Soul

OIL-S: 2343
on page 99

THE
FATHER
THE
SON

The
Soul

THE
HOLY SPIRIT

OIL-S: 2521
on page 101

THE
FATHER

The church

THE
SON
THE
HOLY
SPIRIT

OIL-S: 2528
on page 103

THE HOLY SPIRIT

THE
SON

OIL-S: 2550
on page 105

THE FATHER

The Soul

OIL-S: 2551
on page 107

THE
FATHER

THE
HOLY
SPIRIT
THE
SON

The
soul

OIL-S: 2670
on page 109

THE FATHER
THE SON
THE HOLY
SPIRIT

The soul

OIL-S: 2731
on page 111

```
        THE
        FATHER


THE              THE
SON              HOLY
                 SPIRIT
```

OIL-S:2772
on page 113

```
        THE
        SON
```

OIL-S:3067
on page 115

```
THE      THE      THE
FATHER   SON      HOLY
                  SPIRIT
```

OIL-S: 3105
on page 117

```
The earth

THE HOLY SPIRIT
THE SON


        THE
        FATHER
```

OIL-S: 3198
on page 119

```
        THE FATHER


THE
SON
                THE
                HOLY
                SPIRIT
```

OIL-S: 3247
on page 121

```
        THE FATHER
        The earth
```

OIL-S: 3319
on page 123

```
THE FATHER
    THE SON
    THE HOLY SPIRIT



        Souls
```

OIL-S: 3466A
on page 125

```
        THE
        FATHER

THE              THE
SON              HOLY
                 SPIRIT

        Souls
```

OIL-S: 3466B
on page 127

```
        THE
        HOLY SPIRIT

A                A
soul             soul


        Souls
```

OIL-S: 3768
on page 129

Saints   Saints

THE FATHER
THE SON
THE HOLY SPIRIT

A soul   A soul

OIL-S: 3884
on page 131

THE FATHER
                    The
THE SON   soul

THE HOLY
SPIRIT

OIL-S: 3889
on page 135

                    THE
                    FATHER
            THE
            HOLY
            SPIRIT
THE
SON

OIL-S: 3915
on page 137

THE
SON

OIL-S: 4168
on page 139

THE FATHER
THE SON
THE HOLY SPIRIT

OIL-S: 4174
on page 141

                    THE
THE   FATHER
SON   The   The
      soul   soul

            The   THE
            soul HOLY
                  SPIRIT

OIL-S: 4237
on page 143

THE   THE
FATHER   HOLY
                  SPIRIT

            THE SON

OIL-S: 4270
on page 145

                THE
                HOLY
                SPIRIT
THE
FATHER

            THE
            SON

            The priest

OIL-S: 4299
on page 147

            THE
            FATHER

The   THE
soul SON   THE
              HOLY
              SPIRIT

OIL-S: 4315
on page 149

OIL-S: 4384
on page 151

```
THE
FATHER
THE SON
THE HOLY SPIRIT
```

```
THE
SON

The
soul
```

DETAILS ABOUT THE COMPANY
"RADIANT LIGHT".

The writings and paintings of
Elizabeth Wang are published by
Radiant Light

Radiant Light is a non-profit making company. It has wide trading objects, together with two specific aims which are:

> *'For the glory of God the Most Holy Trinity, for the honour of the Blessed Virgin Mary, and out of love for the Catholic Church and loyalty to the Pope:*

(1) to advance the Roman Catholic religion
(2) to promote the works of Elizabeth Wang

Please write to the Harpenden address below if you would like to be put on the mailing list.

If you would like to help support the work of Radiant Light, please send a UK cheque to **Radiant Light, 25 Rothamsted Avenue, Harpenden, Herts, AL5 2DN.**

Cheques must be made payable to 'Radiant Light'. Thank you.

Company No. 3701357 (Company limited to guarantee and not having a share capital).

Visit the Radiant Light web-site at:
www.radiantlight.org.uk

Book Orders and Distribution.

Radiant Light books, photographs and posters are available from St. Pauls book shop next to Westminster Cathedral, London:

**St. Pauls
(By Westminster Cathedral)
Morpeth Terrace
Victoria
London SW1P 1EP
United Kingdom.**

**Tel: 020 7828 5582
Fax: 020 7828 3329**

email: bookshop@stpauls.org.uk

Mail-Order: If you would like to order Radiant Light works through the post, St Pauls has a very efficient *mail-order service,* which will send your order throughout the UK and anywhere in the world. Please telephone St Pauls and ask them how you may order Radiant Light books. *But please do not send money or orders until you have been in touch with them.*